FINDING PEACE,
the
LAST TASK

Beth Hamilton

Finding Peace, The Last Task
Copyright © 2025 by Beth M. Hamilton

All rights reserved. No part of this book, including icons and images, may be reproduced in any manner without prior written permission from the copyright holder, except where noted in the text and in the case of brief quotations embodied in critical articles and review.

Cover design: Bryana Anderle (YouPublish.com)
Interior design: Sara Hook (YouPublish.com)
Art direction: Chad Harrington (YouPublish.com)

*To my mom, who I miss immensely,
and to my dad, who I couldn't have
written this book without.*

Contents

Introduction 7
Chapter 1 9
Chapter 2 13
Chapter 3 17
Chapter 4 23
Chapter 5 31
Chapter 6 41
Chapter 7 53
Chapter 8 57
Chapter 9 67
Chapter 10 73
Chapter 11 77
Chapter 12 83
Chapter 13 87
Chapter 14 91
Chapter 15 95
Chapter 16 99
Conclusion 101
About the Author 103

Introduction

Curiosity. It can be a very valuable trait, but it can also prove to be an extremely destructive one. Without it, we never push the envelope or seek better, improved ways to accomplish even the most mundane of daily tasks. With it, we sometimes question things that were never meant to be and only require our faith.

I can recall as a young child marveling at the world around me and being overwhelmed by how God could create all of it. How awesome He must be to accomplish so much! Then as I got older, curiosity began to question faith. How does one being do everything Scripture says that God created? Where did He come from? Doesn't something always have to come from something else?

Thus began the journey for answers. This journey would take me to multiple churches, conversations with family and friends, and sometimes just me asking God for answers. It wouldn't be until the end of my mom's life that I would fully understand and comprehend. This book is her story and how each part of her life slowly contributed to strengthening my belief system even if at times it seemed to completely tear it down.

My dad was on a spiritual journey as well, even though his looked somewhat different from mine. We both would share a moment at the end of my mom's life that would join the two separate journeys and help us both find the faith and peace we needed. It is our hope that you as the reader are also able to find comfort from the words on the pages to follow. We dedicate this book to all of the families dealing with loss and especially those who have endured the "long good-bye" know as Alzheimer's Disease.

Chapter 1

Have you ever questioned God's existence? My dad and I had. Life can become what seems to be too much at times. Your faith can be tested to a point of almost no return. Sometimes, something extraordinary must occur to help you see what has always and will always be there. This is what happened to us, and even though it was an arduous journey, I can't imagine changing anything about it. I'm honored to be able to share the story of my mom and the impact she had throughout her life all the way up until her very last breath and beyond.

My mom was born on June 19, 1944 in Mt. Pleasant, Tennessee. She was one of five children, having one older brother, two younger brothers, and one younger sister. She was raised in an extremely strict Church of Christ family. I imagine it was comparable to most families at that time in the small town she lived.

She grew up coming to terms with the "double standard" perpetuated by the local church. While it was okay for her brothers to go to the local swimming pool, it was considered a sin for her to do so. While it was okay for others to wear shorts, it was unacceptable for her to wear them, which almost caused her to fail physical education in junior high school. Dating during high school was not allowed for her while she told me once she was sure her brothers were dating as early as twelve years old, taking their dates to the local theater in the community.

Even though she was quite aware of the differences in how boys were treated versus girls, she loved going to church. Her grandmother provided her with her own Bible when she was a young girl, which now resides on a shelf at my parent's house. You can tell how loved that Bible was. The zipper barely secures a rapidly disintegrating cover enclosing the well-read pages , but oh how it was loved by her. It's my belief this faith that was instilled in her at an early age provided her with the foundation she would need later in life to weather many storms. Looking back now on everything my Mom endured, it's amazing how well she persevered. I realize now what made the difference was her faith and belief in God.

Mom did exceptionally well in school and at times would help her older brother with his classwork. He in turn had incredible artistic ability and would assist her when any of her schoolwork required illustrations or designs. Her innate intellectual ability would serve her well when she became seriously ill in the third grade. Most of her school year would be spent at home in bed. Her dad would help her keep up with her schoolwork to not get behind. This illness almost took her life. She never could tell me exactly what was wrong with her other than the doctor had said she was anemic. She remembered drinking iron through a straw and then eating until her belly hurt but still eating more. While this apparently kept her alive at the time, she fought a weight problem the rest of her life, which she believed could be attributed to the medicine she was given.

Shortly after this, one of her brothers was born prematurely. She remembered her dad saying if her brother would live, he would agree to go to church. There were many times her parents would send my mom and her brothers to church but they would remain at home. Mom said he did attend for a short time after that as her brother did survive, but it was an extremely stressful time in the household. She recounted she would be told to hold her brother and not move. She said it felt like hours that she would be in the rocking chair with her brother in her arms. Also, the house was to be kept as quiet as possible as not to disturb her brother. There were many times she and her brothers would all be disciplined, even if only one of them was responsible for the disturbance or inability to follow the directions of their parents.

By this time, Mom was expected to cook for the entire family. At a young age, she could put a full meal on the table. Not only that, she was responsible for many other household chores. Household chores always came before homework, and she spent many late nights finishing up assignments to be ready for the next day of school. She was also required to make up her own bed and those of her brothers each morning before school. Then she would have to walk to Haylong Elementary School with a stack of books in tow. Mom told me she could remember times she would have to run to make it in time and be exhausted when she arrived with moments to spare. They lived too close to the school for her to be able to ride a bus. This meant no matter whether it was raining or snowing, Mom was out in the weather. At the time, her mother did not have a driver's license, so being taken to school in a vehicle was not an option either. For a time, she was able to roller skate and leave them at her grandmother's house. She described the feeling as almost being able to fly and that it was the best feeling in the world. Finally, she got a hand-me-down bicycle, which she would also have to leave at her grandmother's house and was not allowed to ride all the way to school.

When Mom was sixteen years old, her family moved from Third Avenue to First Avenue, and it was a relief for her with a shorter walk to school. During this time, her sister was born, who was quite the surprise to her parents as my grandmother thought she was going through menopause at the time. Mom took on additionally responsibilities with her sister, and at one point, her sister referred to her as "Mother" because my mom was caring for her as a parent would be. Her younger brother by two years helped out immensely in caring for their sister as well. Mom continued her academic excellence in school and would soon graduate tenth in her class. She was not allowed to attend prom, and during the awards ceremony, she was supervised by my grandmother and great-grandmother, who did allow her to spend the night at her best friend's house to celebrate her graduation.

My mom desperately wanted to attend college to become a teacher. She was awarded a small scholarship for her academic efforts, but it was in no way enough to pay for a four-year degree. Her dad refused to provide her with the monetary resources required. He basically told her she was to find a job because eventually she would just get married and have children. Spending money on a college degree would be a waste of money.

Mom had already worked at a couple of stores in town while attending school and had developed a strong work ethic as well as above-average money saving skills, even though her brothers often tried to "borrow" money without intending to return it. Mom said it was usually to take their dates to the movies while she was still not allowed to date.

Mom was hired for her first full time job but still did not have her driver's license. She had to walk to the bus stop in town each morning to catch the bus into Columbia to her job. After work, she would once again ride the bus back to Mt. Pleasant and walk home. Once she was home, she was expected to cook and clean as usual.

This continued until an unfortunate event occurred on the bus when my mom was hit by another woman's purse for no reason. Her dad finally agreed to let her learn to drive and get her license. Mom told me her driving lessons were very minimal. She laughed about this when telling me, but I'm sure at the time it was very stressful. She said she realized when she got in her car with the person who would be scoring her driving test that she had never backed up a car before. Thankfully, she passed her driving test and no longer had to endure the bus ride to and from her place of work.

Mom had saved enough money to buy her own car, but her dad did not allow her to pick it out herself. He picked one out for her that Mom said was a real "clunker." She said there was no telling how much money she ended up spending on constant repairs. Not only that, but her brothers, who were "borrowers" rather than "savers," always wanted to know if they could use her car as they had been allowed to get their driving licenses well before her. As she would do all of her life, she always made sure her brothers had what they needed, as they did her.

Chapter 2

Not long after this, one of the major life events my mom would have to learn how to emotionally navigate occurred. Her older brother was driving with a friend and hit another car head-on at a high speed. My mom's sister was only a few years old at the time, and the majority of care fell on my mom's shoulders. Her brother would spend weeks in the hospital and would never be able to drive or work again. Due to the severity of his brain injury, he would have seizures for the remainder of his life, even though he was on medication. He did attempt to attend church as he eventually was able to walk wherever he needed to go in the small town, but some members of the congregation voiced their concerns regarding his seizures. They said it scared them and made them uncomfortable, so my uncle quit attending the church. My grandmother, who was emotionally fragile, had an extremely difficult time during this period, and my mom took on many responsibilities so her mother could focus her time and energy on her brother.

Things began to settle down as much as they could, and my mom was out one night with friends (she was finally allowed to date) and met the man who would become her husband, my dad. They met at the Dari-Gem burger joint in Mt. Pleasant and began dating soon after. My dad had just been honorably discharged from the Army and had begun working at a plant in Columbia. There's no other way to put it other than they were soul mates. They were married on September 17, 1966 at her parent's house. On that same day, her younger brother was shipped out to the Vietnam War. It was a day filled with a lot of emotions, both happy and sad.

Not everyone was happy about the marriage. Her sister, who was only six years old at the time, did not realize her sister would be leaving to live with her new husband. My aunt did not like my dad for "taking away" her sister, but the following weekend, he took her for ice cream, and she began to think he might be alright.

Mom continued to do office work during these first years of marriage, and my dad continued to work at the plant. These were tough times. Dad was laid off twice and furloughed for three weeks another time. If they had not worked together, this could have caused an enormous strain on their marriage, but they were dedicated to one another and worked through things other couples might not have been able to handle. Mom and Dad both told me his grandmother had told them marriage was like two horses pulling a wagon. If you both pull in the same direction, you'll go places, if you don't, you'll never get anywhere. How true her words were!

During these years, they were also trying to start a family. This turned out not to be an easy thing for them. My mom would end up having a total of three miscarriages. I always found it odd because she told me once she wanted four children. Finally, after eight years, she became pregnant with me. Earlier, I mentioned she had struggled with her weight due to the medication she received during a childhood illness that almost took her life. Well, before she became pregnant with me, she was in a weight loss management program and reached her lowest adult weight before finding out she was expecting. In order to do this, she only ate tuna fish, apples, and drank black coffee to get down to what would be considered a normal weight for most women. She did this for almost an entire year. When she found out I was on the way, she changed her eating habits to provide me with the best start possible.

On August 24, 1974, I was born. Mom and Dad had discussed it and decided she would be a stay-at-home mom. She had resigned from her job not long after finding out she was pregnant. She went above and beyond when it came to raising me. The only perfume my mom ever wore was White Shoulders. She would spray my sheets in my crib so I could smell her when I slept to help soothe me. She only changed me with clothes that had been warmed prior. Absolutely no "baby talk" was allowed. She would speak to me as she would speak to another adult. I met all milestones incredibly early. My first word was at five-and-a-half months, first steps at seven months, and by eight months, I had decided I was too big for a bottle, so my Mom had taken the nipple off so I could drink directly from it. My parents both said I didn't seem to be a baby for very long.

Not only was Mom learning how to care for a young infant, she also had to juggle my dad's illness. My dad was diagnosed with Meniere's Disease during this time, which is a disease of the inner ear that can result in extreme dizziness and loss of hearing. Right after I was born, he had to go in for surgery to clip a nerve to eliminate the dizziness. He was off from work for a month, so Mom had a newborn and a husband to take care of. My dad said she did a phenomenal job balancing both responsibilities while still keeping up with all other everyday tasks and responsibilities.

The next big life event my mom would have to navigate occurred when I was two-and-a-half years old. She and I had just returned home from getting groceries. Once inside the house, she heard a vehicle in the driveway. It was my dad, and it was too early for him to be home from work. When he came in the house, he let her know her brother had passed away, the same one who had been in the car accident and dealt with seizures for years. My mom said she had sat down on the hearth by the fireplace, and I had walked over to her. Then, I took her hand and said, "Don't worry Mom, he went to heaven." She said I communicated it so emphatically that it caught her off guard, but it was a welcome message.

It was my mom's younger brother who found him. He told her just days before he passed away, their brother told him that "he could see everything so clearly now" and that "he wasn't scared." They were not able to determine if his death was natural or was the result of suicide, but I choose to believe between my message and what my Mom's younger brother told her that regardless how her brother left this world, he was at peace and in his heavenly home.

Chapter 3

In a blink of an eye, it was time for me to go to kindergarten. Mom had already taught me how to set my own alarm clock, make up my own bed, and go retrieve my breakfast from the kitchen. I thought Carnation Instant Breakfast bars were the best thing ever! I'm still upset they quit making those.

The first day of school, Mom walked me in with my breakfast bar, and I took my seat with the other children on the carpet to watch Sesame Street. I was already reading books by this time and really only needed the socialization aspect as I had mainly been around adults up until starting school. Of course, with school came parties. I had never eaten candy up until this point. My mom would give me raisins or treats made with carob. She said everyone got a laugh when I came home from the first party and started emptying my pockets and asked her "what's all this stuff"! Eventually, I did begin to enjoy some of the treats throughout the school year and will never forget when Mom went to the Sweet Shop and purchased cupcakes for the class. I have never and will never taste another cupcake that delicious.

We would return to the Sweet Shop many times over the years. Mom was always looking for ways to make my childhood special and memorable. Some mornings on the way to school, she would surprise me with a trip to the shop, and she would purchase donut twists for my entire class. Other times, she and I would pick out our favorite treat as a special breakfast. I never knew when these trips would occur, but that's what made them so special. She was always looking for ways to brighten someone else's day. Sometimes we even went through a local drive-through to get breakfast biscuits. She always made sure to order one for my teacher too. What wonderful memories we were making!

With me being in school, Mom decided she would volunteer to help out however she could. She had noticed teachers needed help grading papers, students needed help with work they had difficulty learning, and it didn't hurt she could keep an eye on me as well. I imagine it made her feel as if she had somewhat accomplished her desire to become a teacher, even though she never had the funds or opportunity to attend college. I loved having Mom at the school. I felt so important. Teachers would send me on errands to take papers for her to grade or to take a student to her with an assignment they needed extra help with. Mom didn't like it so much. She wanted other children to have opportunities to run errands as well but respected the teachers as professionals and never questioned how they handled her being there. She never wanted anyone to think she was there to spy or pass judgement. She just wanted to help.

Mom also took on the role of room mother. This is something she did every year I was in elementary school. One of my best friends, who ended up being killed in car wreck my senior year of high school, thought the world of my mother. In those days, teachers would take large pieces of chart paper and painstakingly write the names of the students that would be in their class that school year. My friend would go from door to door looking for my name. Now, this was not because he wanted to make sure necessarily that I was in his class; he wanted to make sure he was in the class with the best room mother ever! She was well known for her "party sacks." For any upcoming party, she would go buy various treats to pack the bags with. She made sure every bag had exactly the same items. Occasionally, she would do boy and girl-themed treat bags. My classmates never knew what might turn up in a bag. It could be various types of candy, full-size bottles of bubbles, and one year, every student got a package of sparklers!

The next big life event that would occur for my family would take place during my first grade year. I was to participate in my first school play. The play was to take place prior to Christmas, and I was a sugar plum fairy. My mom, who could also sew (there's not much she couldn't do), made me a beautiful pink ballerina outfit to wear. I was nervous

Chapter 3

but also extremely excited for this new experience. Unfortunately, prior to the play, my mom's dad suffered a heart aneurysm. Thankfully, they were able to get my grandfather to the hospital in time, and he was able to begin his recuperation. However, this meant that Mom was unable to attend. I remember standing on the stage, looking out into the audience, and wishing my mom or dad could be there. My dad had a very demanding job and many people depended on him, so he was unable to attend as well. I persevered through the play and felt a sense of relief and accomplishment when it was over. Mom picked me up from school since we had early dismissal, and we went to my grandparents' house so she could wrap the presents my grandmother had purchased as she had been staying in the hospital with my grandfather. Mom always was there to step up and keep things going whenever needed. My grandfather would be able to come home in time for Christmas to celebrate, and we were all so relieved.

As the years of elementary school began to pass by, Mom would encounter another life-changing event that would place a strain on our family we had never felt before. When I was in the fourth grade, Mom suspected she was pregnant. She felt like something wasn't right, though, and made an appointment with her doctor. During that appointment, Mom would find out two things, and neither was cause to celebrate. Her doctor told her she was most likely in the process of another miscarriage and something was terribly wrong. After tests, it was determined an operation was necessary, and she and my Dad waited for the news.

During surgery, a large tumor was removed and sent off for testing. A panel of physicians reviewed the tests, and my mom was diagnosed with ovarian cancer. She was given less than a ten percent chance of survival. Her medical records were transferred to another doctor and hospital. Mom and Dad made the decision not to tell me. I was only told that Mom was sick and would need additional medicine and doctor visits to treat her illness.

Mom would go every six weeks to Nashville to meet with her doctor and have blood work completed to determine her progress. She would need to undergo chemotherapy. Her readings were so unfavorable that the doctor could only prescribe chemotherapy in pill form. Her body was just too weak to handle anything else at this point I remember watching her take the pill and encase it in sandwich bread before swallowing. She did this as it would burn as she swallowed it and she had found she was able to keep it down longer this way. The longer she could keep the pills in her body, the better chance she had of them working.

During this time, I spent time with both sets of my grandparents. Eventually, my mom's parents started coming over and would be there when I got off of the bus after school. Mom and Dad were trying to keep things as normal as possible for me. Mom was stubborn and would put dinner in the crock pot before leaving for her appointment so my grandparents wouldn't have to worry about trying to cook something. My grandmother would still piddle around the house and do what she could, and my grandfather did the same outside. There really wasn't much to do as my mom, even through her illness, kept the house immaculate.

Mom was on a schedule of when she was to take the pills, and I remember when unfortunately, that schedule fell on Christmas. Mom NEVER complained. We had Christmas at our house that year so Dad could enjoy the festivities and still be by the phone since he was on call. This was, of course, well before the days of the cell phone and answering machine. Mom would work at preparing the meal and every so often would leave the kitchen to throw up before returning to resume where she had left off. Even with all of this, she was in good spirits. Dad loaded up the record player with an assortment of Christmas records, and snow flurries floated down from a gray sky. I remember it as one of my best Christmases, though I'm sure it was one of my mom's most difficult, but she never showed it.

Mom told me years later (she didn't tell me she had cancer until I was in junior high school) that she would lay down at night and imagine shooting each of the cancer cells in her body. Her doctor in Nashville was a man of faith and told her at one of her first visits that they had yet

Chapter 3

to bring in the big guns yet: God. He told he would be asking for God's help and for her, if she felt so led, to do the same, which she did.

Mom required a second surgery. The surgery was designed to complete several biopsies to determine if the cancer had spread to any other parts of her body. Again, I wasn't aware of the severity of the situation as Mom and Dad waited for the news. Thankfully, when the test results came back, there was no trace of cancer in any of the biopsies. Mom had beaten the odds with her faith and determination.

Chapter 4

Mom had continued to volunteer at my school other than the times she had to be out for doctor appointments and hospital stays. Because of her continued support, she was made a lifetime member of the PTA before I left elementary school to move on to junior high. I stop and think sometimes about the amazing impact Mom had throughout those years. There's no telling how many papers she graded, students she assisted, and children she brought joy to by serving as room mother each year. When she got sick, she could have easily said she was too tired and didn't feel well enough to do these things. Not once did I ever hear her complain or turn down an opportunity to help.

Junior high and high school years came and went. Mom was always willing to help me with schoolwork and projects as needed. Her cousin (who was also her best friend) was the librarian at the public library in her hometown, and we would take the short drive whenever I needed to do some research. It would provide Mom with an opportunity to visit too. In my junior year of high school, I got my first job and car. I continued to do well in school, and Mom assisted still as needed until I graduated in 1992, which turned out to be another emotional year.

My senior year of high school, my maternal grandmother was diagnosed with Alzheimer's disease. Many of us had questioned and wondered, and now it had been confirmed by a medical professional. My grandfather still didn't want to accept it, which was completely understandable. He had always relied on my mom to help shop for my grandmother's Christmas gifts, help with holiday meals, etc. He would be reaching out to her more now for support with her mother.

The Christmas of 1998 ended up being a turning point for Mom, though. She mentioned at one point it was, in some ways, the worst

Christmas she had experienced. Her dad called her the middle of December and informed her they weren't having Christmas anymore. His reasoning for this was it was "too much commotion" for her mother. He did still ask her to purchase the gift for her mother as he still wanted to give her something. Mom purchased her mother's gift, wrapped it, and delivered it to her dad. A couple of her siblings did end up stopping by at some point during the holiday, but it certainly wasn't the traditional celebration we had all grown accustomed to. I can say that broke my mother's heart. Christmas had always been one of her favorite holidays. She would thoughtfully buy gifts for each person on her list, beautifully decorate the house, and cook amazing food throughout the season. She never would gain any additional understanding why her dad made that choice. I believe she just chalked it up to her dad navigating her mother's disease and wanting to protect her the best he could.

During those years, I was completing a degree to be an elementary teacher. Mom would be researching ways to fortify herself against Alzheimer's. She would order and read anything she could get her hands on that provided information on how to avoid the disease. She worked crossword puzzles to keep her mind sharp. She looked into various diet plans as to what foods would help reduce the risk of the disease. Years later I would come across many notes she had taken on the subject. She worked so hard to try to make sure she didn't end up the same as her mother.

In the midst of this, I had gotten married, and not long after, my husband and I decided to go ahead and start a family. Additionally, my dad had recently undergone some testing which resulted in finding a polyp in his colon that would require removing a portion of the colon. Mom was not only at this point dealing with me, who was five months pregnant, but also with the worry of her husband going through major surgery.

Mom and Dad continued their strategy of attempting to keep information confidential by not telling me about his upcoming surgery and hospital stay. My pregnancy was not an easy one, and they in no way wanted to add any additional stress. It's interesting how your best plans can be upended in just a few moments, though. I was with my husband at the local grocery store, checking out our groceries for the week. Another couple, who was friends of my parents and I had known since I was a small child, stood in front of us. The man's wife turned to me, and after exchanging the usual pleasantries, mentioned about my dad's upcoming surgery and hospital stay. I didn't know quite how to respond, and bless them, they both looked like deer caught in headlights. I recovered and went along with it as not to make them feel bad. As soon as I returned home, I called my parents, and my mom answered the phone. After I communicated my recent encounter and acquired information, I heard my mom tell my dad in the background, "I told you she would find out"!

What should have been a short stay at the hospital turned into eighteen long days. I think back to how I found out, and all I can come up with was divine intervention. God knew that even though I was dealing with a stressful pregnancy, we would need to pull together as a family to support my dad. Mom stayed strong through it all and finally was able to get my Dad back home and on the mend. She had been a rock for us both as the two of us needed her greatly based on our current conditions. That's what Mom always did, though. She consistently put other's needs ahead of her own.

After a difficult pregnancy and delivery, my son was born in 2000. Unfortunately, my husband and I were not in a place financially where I could be a stay-at-home parent, so after four weeks, I returned to my teaching job. Mom and Dad graciously agreed to keep my son instead of sending him off to day care. There are not enough words to express how blessed I was they agreed to do this. He is the man is he today because of the care, love, and guidance they provided for him during this time. My mom quickly transitioned back into the caregiver she was to me when I was an infant. Additionally, when he was born, one of the first places I took him was to my grandparents' house in Mt. Pleasant. My grandfather was so proud of him, and it was a welcome diversion from the constant care he had to provide to my grandmother. I remember being so sad as he helped her hold their great-grandson. She had such a look of love but at the same time bewilderment. What a cruel, cruel disease Alzheimer's can be.

As my grandmother's disease progressed, most Saturdays, Mom and I would make the drive to her hometown to spend time with her. My grandmother continued a gradual decline, which took a toll on my grandfather. Being the primary caregiver of someone with this disease can be exhausting, no matter how much you love them. He eventually became so sick, my two uncles moved back home to help. In May of 2003, my grandfather passed away in his home.

At this point, my mom took on one of the most stressful roles she had had to this point. She became her mother's conservator. I have often wondered if what she went through mentally had any impact on her own illness later in life. Of course, I can't prove that, but it's just a strong feeling I have based on what I observed over those next years.

It was decided my uncles would continue to live with my grandmother and share the responsibility providing her daily care. My aunt would assist as needed along with my mom. Mom's primary responsibility at this point though was the handling of the financial resources to ensure my grandmother was adequately cared for. My grandfather had made it clear many times before passing that he did not want my grandmother placed in any type of assisted living or nursing home facility. My mom and her siblings agreed to honor his wishes. Mom would be responsible for getting bonded and would be accountable for every cent. At times, she would rely on me to assist with spreadsheets, documenting monthly expenses in the event she was ever questioned by the court. What a tremendous responsibility to undertake, and my mother did it meticulously. Things were about to get a lot harder for my mom though . . .

In March 2004, one of my uncles who had been assisting with my grandmother's care committed suicide. I still remember getting the call from my dad as my three-year-old son stood beside me and looked up

Chapter 4

at me as I got the news. Not only did my mom, her brother, and her sister have to weather the emotions of losing a sibling, they were also now short a caregiver. They would have to revisit the arrangement and determine how best to care for their mother.

The arrangement they decided on consisted of my aunt quitting her current job and taking the day shift, my uncle caring for her during the night, and my mother coming on weekends to assist. Each Saturday morning, my mom would head to the grocery store and purchase the needed items for my grandmother and her household for the week. I went with her on most Saturdays to help however I could.

You learn to do things you never thought you could when you're faced with the care of a loved one. As the days, months, and years passed, I would assist with feeding, bathing, and dressing her. For a time, every time I was at a clothing store, I would pick her up a new nightgown. If it was close to a holiday, I would buy her a holiday-themed one. Mom would laugh about how her mother probably had the best selection of nightgowns of anyone she knew.

My mother continued her research into Alzheimer's and natural remedies to hopefully avoid ending up in the same situation of her mother. We witnessed my grandmother transition through a multitude of behaviors associated with the progression of the disease. Initially, she was very scared and would hide under tables. She was beginning to hallucinate and thought there were strange people in the house. She became resistant to any kind of personal care and bathing. Then she began to exhibit aggressive behaviors. This was completely opposite of who my grandmother was before the disease began to overtake her. I can vividly remember one Saturday when Mom and I were visiting and we were sitting at the table in the kitchen. My grandmother was refusing to keep her house shoes on her feet. My grandfather thought it was chilly in the house and was determined she was going to wear them. As he attempted to put one of her shoes on, she would take the other and hit him over the head with it. It was times like this that were so incredibly sad, but you had to laugh just to keep from crying.

Her aggressive behaviors would continue to increase. Eventually, anything that wasn't too heavy for her to lift had to be removed from her reach or it would be destroyed. She would tear up books, lamps, basically anything she could get her hands on. One day when my aunt was changing her, my grandmother latched on to her dangling earrings and wasn't going to let go. My uncle intervened, and all was well. My aunt did not wear earrings around my grandmother after that occurrence. We were all learning together how to navigate her changing demeanor and needs.

My grandmother eventually became bedridden and non-verbal toward the end of her days of dealing with Alzheimer's. Sometimes she would have faraway looks, and we could only wonder what was going through her mind. At other times, you might get lucky to get a brief chuckle or smile from her. Those were always the best moments, although they were few and far between.

In the midst of continuing to handle all things financial as well as providing help and support directly for my grandmother, my mom would experience another life event that would have us all rattled and concerned. In 2013, my dad was diagnosed with cancer. What had started out as an office visit to remove skin cancer turned into a much bigger ordeal than any of us could have ever anticipated. Unfortunately, the doctor administering the removal of the cancer missed some of the cancer cells.

Dad ended up with a huge cyst on his neck which in turn required a trip to the doctor and the unfortunate diagnosis. He would go through surgery to remove the cyst as well as five weeks of radiation and chemotherapy. Mom not only was researching ways to sustain and improve her own health; she was also researching for my dad. She had determined there were several over-the-counter vitamins and supplements that could help my dad get though the next few weeks of treatments. I had already communicated to my work that I might need to take off to take him to his treatments as they progressed and he could potentially become

Chapter 4

weaker. I am proud to say I never had to take off from work. He drove himself along with my mom to every single visit. Additionally, he never got sick from the chemo. His doctors were amazed and asked if they could have the list of vitamins and supplements he was taking. Mom happily provided them with the information in the hopes of helping other patients in his same predicament. Thankfully, the chemotherapy and radiation worked, and even though dad would need to attend check-ups every three months for one year, he was cancer free!

Chapter 5

In November 2014, my aunt was caring for my grandmother during her day shift and began to recognize the signs that she was passing. She had been in communication with her doctor and knew her time on Earth was coming to a close. She said my grandmother had looked up at the ceiling in the corner of the room and fixed her gaze there. Then the room filled with a beautiful light that just made your soul happy. Moments after, the radiance diminished and my grandmother's long battle with Alzheimer's Disease was finally over.

After serving as her mother's conservator for an unbelievable eleven years, my mom was now able to provide a final accounting of the estate, close all accounts, and conclude this chapter of her life, which had taken an incredible toll on her. It was decided that my uncle would be given the house and what little money remained was divided equitably as it had taken almost all of the money my grandfather had accumulated to take care of her those many years. Thankfully he was good with money, and my mom and her siblings were never faced with running out of funds to take care of her. That was a blessing.

After my grandmother passed, we continued our Saturday morning visits now with my uncle. Any given Saturday the guest list might include myself, my mom, my aunt, my cousin, my uncle's son and his wife, his grandson, and basically anyone driving by in the family who might want to stop by. These would end up being some of my favorite memories, and there was always a good cup of coffee, some type of breakfast treat, and lots of laughter.

After my grandmother's passing, things settled down for a bit. I believe even though Mom felt the loss of her mother being gone, I imagine there was a sense of relief. She had weathered the tremendous responsibility of being her conservator, and those close to her realized what a toll it had taken on her. Mom was an extremely meticulous individual who wanted to make sure everything was as close to perfect as possible, and at times, that turned out to be exhausting for her.

Mom and I were able to return to some of the things we enjoyed doing together with a greater frequency. We were able to resume things like shopping trips, eating out together, stopping to get a sweet treat, and just having time to spend together without the worry of balancing a monthly expense spreadsheet or making out the weekly grocery list for her mother in addition to her own household. Mom and I loved going through the drive-through at a local burger joint and finding a parking place, rolling down the windows, and just enjoying each other's company. Typically, after this, we would go through another one of our favorite places and get an ice cream cone to make the trip complete. Other times, we would visit one of the local stores, whether it be just to browse or fulfill a shopping list we had in hand. Sometimes we would shop together, and sometimes we would split up and agree upon a meeting spot when we had both finished checking out.

Mom had always worked hard at making sure we were able to spend quality time together. During my childhood, I remember how she would stop at the convenience store on the way home and we would both get an Icee. I thought this was just a fun treat, but in actuality, she was slowly teaching and building my independence. Mom would send me in with the money to make the purchase, and then I would bring them out to the car with her change. Of course, there were other things, such as going through a drive-through to just get a root beer or stopping by one of the local shops off of the square so I could get a new pair of fashionable earrings, or just going to a local store to go through the bargain bin of video games. She taught me it didn't take excessive amounts of money to have a good time.

On one of these shopping trips, I noticed something different for the first time. As I had mentioned earlier, Mom and I always had an agreed-upon spot in the event we split up when we were in the store. On

Chapter 5

this particular trip, we agreed to meet at the shopping cart rack, which was inside the store immediately after the checkouts.

I was looking everywhere for Mom. I had walked parallel to all of the aisles, scanning each one as I passed. Mom was nowhere to be found. As a last resort, I headed out to the car to see if she was there, but I didn't think this was likely as she didn't have a set of keys to my car and would just be standing there with her packages. I had parked by a median, which luckily consisted of a couple of trees that provided some limited shade. As I approached where I had parked, there was Mom, standing underneath one of the trees with her shopping bag. She was in a jovial mood and didn't seem distressed in the least bit. I did what anyone might have done in this situation and just explained it away. I don't recall even mentioning the event to my dad. This would be the first of many occurrences that I would attempt to try to justify in some form or fashion until ultimately there was no way the logical, common-sense part of myself could continue to do so.

Looking back to 2015, I do wonder if the following occurrence could have been a sort of foreshadowing of what was to happen to Mom. It was June of that year, and Mom and Dad were doing some renovations on their home. They were replacing the old flooring throughout the house, which put things in disarray for a time. Mom kept an immaculate house, and I believe the anticipation of what it would look like was the only thing that helped her get past the mess. It was the morning the second week of June, and Mom was alone in the house. She had taken a rough fall, apparently tripping where they were working on a portion of the floor. The workers were late getting there that morning, and Mom was hoping Dad would arrive before they did. When he found her, she was on the floor, and she had hurt the entire left side of her body. Dad was able to pick her up. Mom was stubborn and refused to go see a doctor. It was some time before her left shoulder, knee, and ankle would heal. She would continue to have issues with her left wrist for the remainder of her life. Years later when I was reading about how a person in the early stages of Alzheimer's will experience issues with balance, I think to myself maybe this was an early sign we missed. Of course, it could have been just as simple as a hazard in her way that would've caused anyone to trip and fall.

The thing about Alzheimer's is it "sneaks in" and takes over before you truly understand what's taking place. I recall conversations with my dad detailing how it was possible that Mom was just overwhelmed and stressed out. As my job at the time was very demanding, Dad and I made an agreement if there was anything stressful that I needed guidance on or just needed to vent, I would discuss those things with him to give her some breathing space. After a time, we realized this strategy would have no positive effect on the current situation.

We began to notice that when she brought in the groceries, items that should have been stored in the refrigerator would end up stored in cabinets. That can happen to anybody, right? I've caught myself attempting to place items in the wrong spot because I had my mind on other things. The difference is I would realize what I was doing, and the item would end up properly stored. He and I also observed that even when we had items, she would end up buying them every time she went to the store even though we didn't need them. Again, we chalked it up to it never being a bad thing to be stocked up just in case.

During this time, Mom was still researching ways to fortify herself against Alzheimer's Disease. Quite often when I went over to visit, I found her reading on the subject or jotting down some notes, or possibly ordering a supplement that professed to sharpen one's cognitive abilities. I've thought back to these times and wondered if she suspected there was something wrong or was still just in the thought process that she was going to continue to research and do whatever was within in her power to make sure she didn't end up the same way her mother did.

I can remember vividly the day I finally resigned myself to accept that what was occurring with Mom was more than the occasional forgetfulness. I was on the phone with my mom's sister one afternoon and finally mustered up the courage to ask her if she had noticed anything about Mom that would indicate or cause her to believe some of her

Chapter 5

behaviors were reminiscent of my grandmother's behavior at the onset of Alzheimer's. I honestly heard somewhat of a sigh of relief in her voice. Her answer would confirm that we were both in agreement that Mom was exhibiting signs of the disease. I believe she had wanted to broach this topic before, but I imagine she wanted to wait until I ready to talk about it.

After this conversation, I tried to talk to my dad about it, but he still was not convinced that Mom was in the initial stages of Alzheimer's. I did not argue with him as I know from personal experience, if you're not ready to accept or discuss something, there's no reason to belabor the point. I knew there would come a time when he would be ready to talk, and for the moment, I left it alone. Also, there was also that little voice telling me maybe, just maybe my aunt and I were both wrong.

I vividly recall the day Dad finally reconciled himself to the fact that Mom was indeed displaying the characteristics of Alzheimer's Disease. We had gone to town together, and he was dropping me off at my house. Before I started to open the door to the truck, he told me we needed to talk a minute. He told me that he agreed that Mom's issues went beyond that of normal aging and forgetfulness. He told me we'd have to be tough because he imagined it would be a long road and we'd both need to be there for her. And that was it. Later, he would tell me what opened his eyes was he offered to go with Mom to the grocery store to help her with the shopping. He said she was consistently putting things in the shopping cart that they had more than enough of at home. When he tried to correct her about it, she became extremely argumentative to the point he just let her put whatever she thought they needed in the cart. He said it just wasn't worth arguing over. Now Dad and I were on the same page, and thus began the long goodbye that would be one of the toughest things we had endured but also one of the most positively life-changing as well.

We quickly found that you really can't compare one person's Alzheimer's journey with that of another. We had already lived through my grandmother's Alzheimer's stages, but while some of the symptoms and behaviors would be similar, others would be as different as day is from night.

The signs of Alzheimer's started out small. Dad would find yogurt stored in the cabinet instead of the refrigerator. Mom would have difficulty recalling the name of a relative she didn't see often but had kept in touch with over the years. We had numerous discussions on whether or not she should still be driving, but Dad wasn't ready to take that away from her yet since she'd had no problems recalling the way to and from local destinations. He kept a close eye on her and took her to town as often as he could. You realize your loved one is losing a little piece of themselves every day, and you hate to intentionally take anything else away from them.

It was not a significant event, I recall, when Mom stopped driving. Dad had increased the frequency of accompanying her to and from town, so I believe it just turned into a natural progression of the transfer of responsibility. Anything he could do to make this less traumatic for her, he did without a second thought. He made sure the keys to the car were no longer accessible to her for her protection. He knew it was to the point that it was quite possible if she drove to town, she could potentially panic, not remembering how to get back home.

During this time, she also stopped several things she had always excelled at, which were embroidery, sewing, and cooking. Mom was famous with friends and family for her embroidered pillowcases as well as her Raggedy Ann and Andy dolls. If Mom was going to do something, she was going to do it meticulously, and I'm thankful I have these items in my own home as a cheerful reminder of her handiwork. Also, over the years she had compiled recipes to make her own recipe book. She had put hours into its creation. Every recipe was neatly typed and categorized for ease of access. My love of cooking comes from years of watching her entertain friends and family for various occasions and observe them absolutely enjoying each morsel they put in their mouths. As the disease progressed, she didn't let her embroidery thread or her cookbook get too far from her. In one of the stages, I knew when I stopped by after work, I could count on her proudly showing me her cookbook. Sometimes she would tell me she did it when she was in the third grade while other times it was a creation from junior high as a class requirement. You gradually learn to not correct and smile and enjoy the moment with your loved one wherever they are currently in their mind.

For a time, Mom was able to microwave to assist with meal preparation. I remember when Dad and I both realized that was no longer an option. He had been outside working in the yard when I had come over for a visit. When I went into the kitchen, I just felt like something wasn't right. I heard the microwave running and when I glanced over, I noticed she had put over forty minutes for the cooking time. From that point forward, Dad would be handling food preparation. He still tried to help her by assigning tasks such as cutting up vegetables, peeling eggs, or washing up the dishes. She was always eager to help as I believe it helped her feel important and needed.

As a resource for additional household income, my dad had always raised Black Angus cattle in addition to working at a local plant. When he wasn't at the plant, you could find him servicing his tractors, working on various equipment, cutting/raking/baling hay, or working the cattle. Even though this was all certainly hard work, it served as an outlet for him as his full-time job was very demanding and stressful at times. As Mom continued to progress through the stages of Alzheimer's, it became increasingly evident that she would require constant supervision. So Dad made the difficult decision to sell off all of his cattle and some equipment. He would keep his tractor so he could keep the pasture clipped when needed. He and I would typically determine a date/time that worked for us both and I would sit with Mom while he got out on the tractor. It was difficult for me to see this happen as I had fond memories of my childhood of bottle-feeding calves, hauling in hay, feeding the cows, and many more tasks too numerous to name. As hard as this was for me, I knew it was that much harder for my dad. It occurred to me on several occasions that Dad had basically become a prisoner in his own home. We both loved her dearly, but entertaining the idea of assisted living was not something either of us was ready to discuss.

During this time, Dad also realized he would have to give up his weekly golf outings with his friends. I hated for him to have to do this, but at this point, there were no other options. I did my best when I had vacation days to watch Mom so he could get out and go golfing. I think sometimes when people get married and recite their vows, they don't truly have an understanding of what "for better or worse" entails. As difficult as these times were, the most important thing was we loved her and wanted to do everything we could to make the best of a terrible situation that we knew would never get better but only worse.

I would still take Mom out during this time. Granted, we didn't split up in the store anymore. We were well beyond that. We would usually take a trip to visit her brother, who still lived in their childhood home. Usually when we visited, Mom always made sure to stop and get a breakfast biscuit to enjoy for everyone who would be stopping by . I had chosen to continue this tradition and told Mom we would stop on the way. In transit to the drive-through, Mom tried to give me money to pay. She had developed a habit of going through her purse and taking everything out and then putting it back in. If she knew I would be spending money on something, she would repeatedly try to pay for whatever it was. She would take out her wallet and look through all of the various compartments. When she found the money, she would desperately attempt to give it to me. This conversation was basically on a loop. At first, it was frustrating, but eventually you learn to develop patience, and sometimes the technique of redirection can be effective as well. I learned never to argue or disagree as that only caused the situation to worsen.

Part of the progression of Alzheimer's is the person loses the keen concept of dealing with money. Mom had always been known as "the budget woman." For years she kept immaculate financial records, and when it came to tax time, she had kept all of their receipts and totaled the amount of taxes paid for the maximum tax return. Dad always credited her with how well off they were financially. They had managed to pay off their house years ahead of schedule because of Mom's meticulous budgeting techniques. Now, Mom struggled with a task as simple as balancing a checkbook. Dad had locked up her checkbook, check card, etc. He did leave her twenty dollars to keep in her wallet. He just didn't think it was fair to take everything away from her.

Chapter 6

During this stage of Mom's Alzheimer's, even though there were noticeable differences in her behavior, Dad and I were happy as long as she was happy. Our main hope was that she would never become angry or scared. We could handle the inability to complete daily tasks as she had in the past. Additionally, we could navigate the loss of memory. If she could continue in this manner with a sense of joy, peace, and happiness, we could experience that same joy, peace, and happiness too.

Mom would be able to continue in this stage for several years. I guess you could say we were in somewhat of a holding pattern. Small steps were taken as needed. Once we realized she was forgetting who more and more people were in our family, Dad made the wise decision of placing all of our family photograph albums in the safe. He had read somewhere that people with Alzheimer's will come across those photos, and when they don't recognize anyone, they will simply tear them up or throw them away. You really do lose a little bit of your loved one every day.

One thing Mom did continue to consistently enjoy was sitting on the back deck my dad had built for her. Several years earlier, Mom and I had taken my dad's truck and ventured to the local home improvement store. She and I had picked out a swing as well as an outdoor table with chairs. The items were loaded into the back of the truck and secured with rope. I don't think either one of us breathed too deeply until we arrived back at her house as we both were not completely sure the contents were tied down as securely as we would've liked. My dad and I unloaded the truck and began the tasks of unpacking and assembling. She was so proud of her furniture. I can't even begin to count the times we spent on that back deck, enjoying one another's company.

Sometimes, she would sit on the swing while my dad completed outdoor tasks such as mowing the yard, tilling the garden, etc. If it was warm enough when family and friends stopped by for a visit, she always preferred to visit with them on the back deck.

This would also turn out to be the location of her first major decline. My aunt had come over to visit, and she and I were lounging in chairs while Mom was seated on the swing. When we were getting up to go back into the house, she fell. Mom's knees were not in the best shape, which I believe may have been a result of the previous chemotherapy treatments. We don't really know exactly what happened as everything occurred so quickly, but Dad and I believe one of her knees may have buckled, causing the fall.

It was obvious at this point that she was in great pain. She was adamant that she did not want to go to the hospital, but we were unsuccessful in getting her up due to her protesting in pain, so we knew something was terribly wrong. I went in the house to call 911 for an ambulance and asked them to not use their siren as it most likely would cause Mom even more agitation.

When they arrived, they quickly ascertained that she indeed had done some sort of damage to herself and gave her shots for the pain and the extreme anxiety she was experiencing. It broke my heart to see her this way. It was bad enough she was dealing with Alzheimer's, but now she had a whole separate challenge to deal with. We followed the ambulance to the hospital, and after testing and x-rays were completed, it was determined she had broken her hip and would require surgery.

Dad was exhausted, and we decided I would stay with her that night at the hospital. I don't think either one of us slept that night. At one point I could've sworn she was talking about floating above herself and seeing herself in the bed. The night consisted of constantly reassuring her that everything was going to be okay and that even if it didn't feel like it right now, she would be feeling better soon. She kept asking what had happened over and over. She just couldn't keep what had happened in her mind, and to make it worse, she was in a strange place.

Chapter 6

Mom and I made it through the night, and she was taken to surgery the next morning. Dad came back out to the hospital, and we waited together for her to come out of surgery. Mom made it through the surgery, and then we were quickly faced with many decisions that had to be made in a short time.

Mom's hospital stay was a complicated one to say the least. Her accident occurred during the height of the COVID pandemic. The hospital had extremely rigid rules for visitors, which my Dad and I completely understood except for one issue we encountered. They did not want more than one family member with their loved one during a twenty-four-hour period. That meant they expected Dad to stay for a full day, and then he could trade off with me and I could do the same. We pushed back. We both were already exhausted. In addition, I was still trying to work remotely so I wouldn't get behind at my job. I don't know if the medical professionals ever actually agreed to us changing out every twelve hours, but at least they never confronted us about it. I truly believe they didn't because one of the nurses on staff really didn't want to deal with Mom.

One day when it was my shift, I needed to step out for a minute to do a Zoom conference with one of my employees. I informed the nurse I would be out of the room for five to seven minutes and then I would return. She told me to make sure to hurry back. When I re-entered the room, the nurse was not happy. Mom had apparently been a handful while I was out of the room for just a matter of mere minutes. Mom was known for trying to pull out her IV and catheter due to high anxiety because of the confusing situation and setting. The nurse informed me it was my responsibility to watch her and that she couldn't be running in the room to check on her. Now, I understand nurses have a lot of responsibilities and that it's completely possible to be easily be overworked, but bottom line, Dad and I chose to be there to help. It was in no way a requirement of her stay. For goodness sake, she was dealing with a broken hip and Alzheimer's.

I chose to ignore the nurse and her actions the best I could and tried to keep my focus on Mom. I requested that she be administered medicine to assist with the high anxiety and hopefully help her to get some sleep and rest. The nurse reluctantly agreed to contact Mom's doctor, and we were finally about to get her the medicine and some much-needed rest. The rest of the medical professionals Dad and I encountered were extremely helpful and understanding. We were very grateful for that.

During Mom's stay in the hospital, she developed another issue: arterial fibrillation. At this point it was decided she would need additional medication to address this recent issue and her discharge was delayed. Ah . . . the discharge. That became another ordeal that Dad and I would have to navigate. The medical staff recommended that she be transported to a skilled nursing facility once leaving the hospital. They really couldn't give us a timeline of how long she would need to be there because of the Alzheimer's. Mom and Dad had never really been apart from each other over the years other than a few nights here and there for a business trip for Dad or when my mom had to help take care of her mother. Dad and I discussed it, and he wanted to bring her home. I told him if that was what he wanted, we would figure out a way to make it work.

First, the medical staff that entered the room that day to discuss next steps began to talk about the particulars in front of Mom as if she was a child who wouldn't really pay attention to the conversation. Up until her last days, Mom still had some sharp skills even though other parts of her memories were fading. I directed them to the hallway and as politely as I could, I requested they not discuss these things in front of my mother since she understood more than what you would expect and this would cause her additional anxiety that she certainly didn't need. I told them my dad and I had decided to bring her home with home-based services as needed such as physical therapy. They vehemently argued with me, but I didn't back down. They did not mince words with me and said he and I would never be able to provide the care for her that she would need/receive in a skilled nursing facility. I let them know at this point, it was not their decision to make and my mom was coming home. It was one of the times in my life when I felt completely talked down to, and

Chapter 6

I knew in my heart we would most emphatically show them they were wrong and had greatly underestimated us.

Plans were made to transport Mom home. Her transport was not considered "medically necessary" even though she was still having difficulty standing and even taking a few steps. I wanted to fight this, but Dad and I were intent on saving our energy for when Mom got home. Her brother agreed to meet us and spend some time with her. I followed the ambulance to my parents' house, and Mom was returned to familiar surroundings. She was so happy! We obviously had a long road to travel, but this was a first confirmation that the decision we had made was the right one. My mom and her brother visited together that morning, and laughter could be heard throughout the house. Now the hard work of recovery from the fall would begin.

The first nights, Mom was extremely restless. In a way this was good as she was moving, but I hated she couldn't seem to get settled. The job Dad retired from required a tremendous amount of problem solving, and he put those skills to good use when dealing with Mom. Soon we had a system down to help her get from the bed to her chair in the living room. I had mastered helping her with things such as going to the bathroom, getting dressed, etc. If you had asked either my Dad or myself several years before this if we thought we could ever provide this level of care, we probably would've been unsure or vague with our response. Thankfully, we found the strength within ourselves to be there for her for what she needed. When you love someone as much as we loved her, you'll amaze yourself with the things you never thought you'd be able to do.

Mom did not like physical therapy. There was nothing wrong at all with the individuals that came to the house, but Mom felt differently. I can recall the first visit to the house. Dad and I let Mom know someone would be coming by and there were just there to help. She responded by saying, "I don't need any help." We acknowledged her response and advised her to just to go along with whatever they asked. We let her know they would not hurt her, and we of course would be there if she needed anything.

The visit started with the usual questions. Mom did not remember falling, nor did she recall the hospital stay, or anything associated with the surgery. When she had difficulty moving around, she would theorize she had done too much work, moved wrong, etc. We would remind her that she had broken her hip. She would say, "I broke my hip? How in the world did I do that? Are you sure?" We would go through this multiple times a day.

After the questions, the physical therapist would get Mom out of her chair and use the safety belt. She certainly did not like this. When the physical therapist couldn't see her face, she would share with us expressions that clearly communicated that someone had lost their mind and it wasn't her. You have to do your best to find as much humor as you can in these situations, and it was hard not to laugh. Mom didn't want to hurt anyone's feelings, though, and would reluctantly agree with whatever their request was and would sometimes look to us for confirmation all of this was okay.

Additionally, they provided us with exercises Mom could complete on the days they were not scheduled to visit. We kept them posted on the refrigerator in the kitchen as she could hold on to the edge of the counter to perform them. I would do them alongside her to model what was expected, and that seemed to work well. She almost seemed to have a sense of pride of how well she was able to execute these exercises, and of course there was no lack of affirmation and encouragement from Dad and me.

Miraculously, Mom completed all of her physical therapy at home and had healed well from the broken hip. There were several times I wished I could have been able to speak to the group of medical professionals who told me that Dad and I would never be able to handle her at home. It there were ever a time I wanted to say, "I told you so!", it was then.

Chapter 6

After recovering from the injury, Mom developed a new hobby. She had a never had a lazy bone in her body and she wasn't going to begin to now. Any time she had an opportunity to get outside with Dad, you would find her doing one of two things. First, she would locate a broom and sweep every leaf, acorn, or speck of dirt she could locate off of the back deck, concrete parking area, or driveway. She didn't miss anything! Another thing she took pride in was helping Dad with the yard before he would mow. Dad always made sure all of the fallen limbs, branches, and twigs from the trees in the yard were picked up so as not to dull the blade on the lawnmower. Mom was a pro at doing this. She would not stop until the job was complete. She amazed me at how she could bend over at the waist and would've easily been able to touch the ground with both her hands. By the time she was finished, you would've needed a magnifying glass to find anything else. Both Dad and I would try to get her to slow down or rest, but neither one of us were very successful. And another thing, she was happy. I believe somewhere in her mind, she realized there were things she couldn't do any more like balancing the checkbook or cooking biscuits from scratch. So, when she found something she could do and knew it made someone else's job easier, she took great delight in that.

There was one problem that came with this, though. We noticed that Mom was picking up some of the acorns and putting them in her pocket. When Dad saw this, he would tell her she didn't need to bring them in the house and they needed to be left outside. Confused, she would agree and let him have them. Unfortunately, we didn't always catch these moments, and Mom was quick. I don't know how she did it sometimes, but the only way I know to describe it is like when you turn your back on a small child for just a second and then they've gotten into something they didn't need to be in. So sometimes, these acorns made their way into the house. We would find them in her sewing basket, wrapped in tissue in drawers, and Dad would go through all of her pockets when doing the laundry and find them there as well.

At the time, we thought Mom was only collecting these, but on a couple of occasions, she had gotten sick to her stomach. Dad was baffled as he handled all of the food preparation and was very careful with expiration dates on food. Even though we couldn't say with one hundred percent certainty this is what had caused her upset stomach, we were fairly sure she had attempted to eat some of the acorns. We both became pretty adept at making sure those acorns no longer made it in the house.

It was a fact that Mom's eating habits had definitely changed. Prior to Alzheimer's, she would only eat sweets on special occasions or when occasionally we would go through McDonald's and get a milkshake or ice cream cone. She did not normally keep a lot of sweets in the house and had always been careful with this. My dad, of course, had taken over all of the grocery shopping and had starting picking up oatmeal crème pies pretty regularly along with dark chocolate candy. Mom found a great love for both. He eventually had to hide them as she was going back multiple times a day to get another crème pie or piece of candy. What was kind of humorous about the situation though was if you asked her if she ate a lot of sweets, she would emphatically state that she didn't eat a lot of those. Dad and I would just exchange a glance and chuckle.

When Mom had been discharged from the hospital, she had also been discharged with a couple of medications. One was a blood thinner due to the atrial fibrillation she experienced after her surgery. Dad and I quickly found out how expensive this medication turned out to be. We certainly were going to make sure she got the medical care she needed, but this particular drug had potential of depleting financial reserves sooner rather than later. We consulted with her doctor and were able to find another medication that was comparable. There was only one catch with it though. She would have to come in sometimes as often as weekly to have her blood tested to adjust the medication as needed.

Mom did not like going to the doctor at all. Dad would typically tell her they were just going to run a few errands or just getting out for a drive. He would then "swing by" the doctor's office and tell Mom they

Chapter 6

would go in quickly and be back out before she knew it. He was pretty convincing with how he sold this to Mom, and even though she was reluctant at times, she mostly was cooperative. She didn't understand why they had to make these visits as she was "just fine" according to her. She was always so pleasant with everyone when she went in for these visits. She never wanted to hurt anyone's feelings and always tried to be a good patient and do exactly what they asked her to do as long as she knew she wasn't going to be there very long. The few occasions I took her for these visits, I found it helpful to tell her we'd grab a breakfast biscuit after, and that seemed to give her something else to look forward to, even if it only stayed in her memory for mere moments.

Mom continued the medication and visits until we observed that she seemed to be in decline and potentially transitioning to the next stage of the disease. I inquired with her doctor regarding hospice care, and the process was initiated. One of the intake nurses came out to the house and as not to upset Mom, we went out on the back deck since it was a nice day so I could complete her questionnaire. I believe that was the first time the reality of everything had really sank in for me. It was difficult to stay stoic answering some of the questions. Mom and Dad both had already created their wills before Mom had gotten sick, and I clearly knew their wishes regarding medical measures covered in the legally binding documents.

After answering all of the questions to the best of my ability, the nurse stated that Mom did meet the necessary requirements for hospice care. That day it was determined that no extreme measures were to be taken to save my mother's life. The nurse did decide Mom would continue to take her blood pressure medication, but the blood thinner was stopped immediately, mainly because she was a continued fall risk and that particular medication could potentially cause internal bleeding in the event she did take a bad fall. No longer did Dad have to find ways to convince her of why they needed to go to town, and Mom no longer had to endure the sometimes-weekly visits to determine medication dosages.

One of the things we had learned about patients that have Alzheimer's is they really don't like showers or baths. I don't know why that is, but hygiene becomes a huge issue. This was a complete 180 from how my mom was before the disease took ahold of her. Part of hospice was providing her with assistance with bathing, but my mom was having no part of it. The ladies who came out to the house were so thoughtful and understanding as well as patient. They tried so hard with her, but for this part of the current stage she was in, it was hit or miss if you could talk her into it. Dad was usually more successful than any of us. He would tell her that she had asked him to remind her that she was going to take a bath that day and he was just doing what she had asked. That worked for a while until it didn't. She would tell us that she had just taken a bath, and we would respond that we didn't find any used towel or washcloth. Then her response would be that was because she already done the laundry (which my Dad did now). You had to give Mom credit. Even though her memory was diminishing, she had a mean skill set! Dad even went as far to install one of the walk-in spa tubs for her. I believe she only used it twice. He tried as hard as he could to make things as accessible and easy for her as possible. She was just hard to reason with at this point.

Then what we had been able to avoid up until this point happened. Mom was now showing signs of being afraid. This is the one thing we both never wanted to happen to her, but I guess looking back now, it was just unavoidable. I can remember one day when I stopped by to see her, she was seated in the living room with Dad. He decided he would go out and do some work in the garage. As soon as he left out of the house, Mom looked at me and asked me if I knew who that man was. I told her that I did. I didn't say anything additional yet because I wanted to know from her perspective what she was thinking. She went on to say that he was "very nice", but she really should be getting back home as her parents would be wondering where she was.

When Dad and I first started noticing this type of behavior from Mom, we did attempt to fill in her memory gaps. It worked for a while.

Chapter 6

If she didn't know who Dad was, I would explain that was her husband and he was my Dad. I would tell her how long she had been married, how long she had lived in the house, etc. Dad would do the same. We eventually typed up a one-page paper with all of her information listed where she could read it herself. This worked for a while. Eventually, her memory got to the point that the paper no longer brought her any peace or understanding.

We reached a point of where all she wanted to do was to go home. We had gradually observed her go backwards in time. Based on communication with her, you could pretty much determine where she was mentally regarding the timeline of her life. Even through all of this, when Dad would ask her who I was when I would come over in the afternoons after work, she would say, "Beth Marie." When asked who I was to her, she would say I was a "good friend." She no longer remembered getting married or having me. So many of her life events were lost to her with no hope of ever gaining access to them again. It's so sad to see someone robbed of some of their best memories. I know during this time, Dad and I questioned our faith as we wondered how could such a caring God let this happen to such a wonderful human being who already been through so much and fought so hard not to have this type of outcome.

Some of the times when she would start talking about going home, she would be very emphatic about how she was going to get in her car and head back home. We both tried to reason with her, but it really wasn't possible. Dad had made sure the keys to any of the vehicles were out of her reach for her safety. Typically, interactions such as these would eventually end with her giving up and going to bed. Sometimes Dad would be able to convince her it was too dark to head home and she could get up the next morning and head home when it wouldn't be so difficult to see. This would work sometimes too. Of course, by the next morning, she would have no recollection of the conversation. To be honest she probably didn't remember what had been said within the hour.

One thing remained constant though. She still kept the cookbook she was so proud of close by. At one point, she actually stored it under the bed in her bedroom. It was very important to her. I believe she kept focus on it because cooking was something she had done since she was a young girl, so it had almost always been a part of her life. She even tried to still put a dinner together at times. Eventually, we had to order a key to keep the freezer locked so she wouldn't take food out and put on the counter or fridge. The Mom I knew before Alzheimer's took a hold of her would've been mortified to know she was doing this.

Chapter 7

Other things we did to try to help with her anxiety would be to drive her to where she had lived growing up. The only way Dad was able to calm her down one evening was to drive her all the way to her previous house in Mt. Pleasant. When he pulled in the driveway, he pointed out some things about the house that were different from the time when she lived there. She finally agreed with him that her parents most likely were not there and they returned home. On another occasion, I drove her around and we went past the two houses she lived in when she was a girl. Things had changed so much that it was hard for her really to connect with the locations. At this point, any time we had her out she would rarely recognize any surroundings and basically just have a look of confusion.

I recall the last trip we took to Mt. Pleasant to visit her brother. I drove through the back yard and pulled around to the side of the house because her knees wouldn't allow her to navigate the front steps very well. When we entered, my cousin and his wife as well as her childhood friend, sister, and brother were all there to greet us. She went into the living room to visit with her brother and friend while the rest of us visited with one another at the kitchen table. We of course had brought breakfast biscuits for everyone, and it was one of the best mornings I can remember in some time for Mom. She and her brother especially chatted away, and laughter could be heard throughout the house. I could sense the sadness when it was time to leave. It was obvious she felt comfortable there and connected with it as more of a home than the one I was about to drive her back to. Even though we were leaving, she was in really good spirits for the drive back. Those were the kind of days that made me feel as if a glimmer of who my mom used to be was still there.

As I quickly found out with my dad, just because one spouse is dealing with health issues doesn't mean that the other spouse will magically be free of any health concerns. That's when it was time to let everyone know it's "all hands-on deck" to make sure everyone is taken care of. Dad had become extremely sick but, being extremely stubborn, had tried to "power through" whatever the ailment was. He got to the point that he realized this was no longer a viable option. I reached out to my son, who came over to take him to the emergency room late one evening while I stayed with Mom. It was the divide and conquer strategy that I will never forget.

Dad had told me I could lie down in his room, and Mom's was directly across. I could listen and hear her if she needed anything or got up in the middle of the night as she sometimes did. I had made sure she was lying down in her room, and I told her I would be just across the hall in Dad's room if she needed anything at all. She was confused and upset, which was understandable especially since nighttime is the most challenging part of the day for an Alzheimer's patient. I had not been lying down very long when Mom came to the door and said I could lay down with her if I needed to and wanted to know if I needed anything. As my husband has said, I'm known for my snoring, so I declined because I wanted her to be able to hopefully get some rest. This went on several more times, so I finally gave up and went in the living room to sit in one of the recliners and watch TV. What happened next was nothing I could have ever been prepared for.

Mom could move through the house like a ninja at times, and this was one of those times. I looked up from my chair to see her standing in the doorway of the living room, and she did not look happy. What happened next is something we can laugh about now, but at the time I was completely mortified. She accused me of sleeping with her husband. She did not recognize me as her daughter. She said I "was cute" and he would "like that." My jaw dropped out of pure astonishment. Did I really hear what I just think I did?

Chapter 7

She was like a dog with a bone and she was not letting this go. It took over an hour of me reassuring her that I had no intention of what she was talking about and that since I was their daughter, this was not a possibility in the least. I told her she was confused and mistaken about what she was perceiving. After repeating myself multiple times, she finally started to relent. Eventually she even went as far to say that I seemed like a "good person," and she guessed I wouldn't do anything like that.

Finally, my son and Dad returned from the ER in the early hours of that next morning. Dad had an infection; they were able to administer the medication through an IV, and he was to make an appointment with his doctor. Thank goodness it hadn't been anything worse. When I told him about what had occurred, he busted out laughing. I have to admit, I was still somewhat traumatized from the earlier conversation with my mom, but it was good to see Dad laughing instead of throwing up. What an evening it had been!

The holiday season was now in full swing, and Christmas was rapidly approaching. Mom had continued to decline, and most days had her wanting to go home and worrying if her parents knew where she was. I would stop by almost every day after work, and if Dad had redirected as much as he could withstand at the moment and I wasn't there, he would call me on the phone to try to help. Sometimes it worked, and sometimes it didn't. You never really knew how Mom was going to respond. She simply did not remember the home she was currently in and wanted to be back at her childhood home with her parents. It was heartbreaking.

Chapter 8

It was an early Monday morning in December when I received a phone call from Dad. Mom had fallen, and he had reached out to hospice and one of the nurses on call was on her way. One of the things we learned early on about hospice was we were to call them first and then they would make the determination if the patient required hospital care or not. When I got there, Mom was on the floor beside of her bed, and no matter how hard she tried, she could not get up off of the floor. Dad had heard her from the other room when she fell and rushed in to see what had happened. The hospice nurse arrived not long after I did. After quickly evaluating her, she determined an ambulance would need to be called as she was quite certain Mom had broken some bones. She made the call, and we waited on the emergency personnel to arrive.

It was a difficult task to get Mom off of the floor, and we could tell she was in immense pain as she was lifted onto the stretcher. Dad was exhausted by this point, and I could tell he was blaming himself for the fall. I hated that since all Dad had ever done was provide Mom with the very best care possible. He had everything running like clockwork. Her meds were always administered at the same time each day. She was provided with meals on a regular schedule, and he watched her like a hawk. You simply can't be everywhere at all times, and I was so proud of how diligent he had been in taking care of her and watching over her. Unless you've been in someone's shoes like that, you cannot even begin to imagine the enormous responsibility of caring for someone with this disease.

Mom was transported to the hospital, and I followed behind the ambulance. Dad and I decided he would try to get some rest, and I would call to provide him with updates about Mom and go from there. The hospice nurse let me know one of their case workers would be out at the hospital to sit with me and help me navigate the situation. I also reached out to my mom's sister, and she joined me at the hospital as well.

My aunt and I were sitting with my mom in her room in the emergency area when the hospice care worker arrived. I excused myself to go discuss what had happened and did something I normally didn't do. I fell apart. I didn't feel like I was much help to Mom at this point, and I had called in to work to let them know I wouldn't be in, and so in a sense I felt like I was letting my work family down as well. It was the most hopeless feeling. The case worker was wonderful. She listened intently, ignored her phone when it went off, and basically gave me her undivided attention. They had taken Mom back for x-rays, so we would soon know what we were dealing with and could determine next steps.

When the doctor returned, she communicated what I had feared. Mom had not only broken her hip, but she had also broken her wrist. The doctor was very upfront with me that they would need to go ahead perform surgery to address both the hip and the wrist but to be prepared that patients with her challenges cognitively do not typically make it longer than six months. I called Dad to let him know, and I remember him saying, "I guess we've had the best of her, haven't we?" How true those words turned out to be. It was the beginning of the end.

As they prepared to take Mom to a hospital room, I navigated the other aspects of the current reality. I would have to suspend hospice care and return to her previous insurance that thankfully Dad had chosen not to cancel. It's not enough that you have to deal with what's going on emotionally; you have to make sure you have everything covered with insurance, and we were fortunate we had not canceled her previous insurance. No one really tells you anything, and you feel at times as if you're just doing things by guess and by golly.

When Dad arrived at the hospital and visited with Mom, he could tell she was really out of it. The doctors were currently trying to determine the best way to address her wrist as, being an Alzheimer's patient, she of course would not remember what had happened. The hip was a little easier to deal with. I recall waiting with her for her surgery and

Chapter 8

praying for peace for her and the rest of my family. I remember her telling me she just wanted to go home. It was so incredibly sad. I had taken her wedding ring and was wearing it on my own hand until I could get it back to Dad. All of the years I was growing up, I never once recalled my Mom taking off her wedding band unless it was for a surgery.

As the surgery began, Dad and I didn't know what to expect. We were told there was a possibility she wouldn't make it through the surgery, but she could also come through it with no issues. You basically just brace yourself for any scenario or outcome. Mom did make it through the surgery with no major issues. What we didn't realize at the time but would quickly find out was in order to address the issue of her wrist, the doctor had chosen to place a pin in her wrist. This would turn out to be one of the most challenging parts of her recovery. We met with the doctor, and he communicated as far as the technical aspect of the surgery, he was very pleased with how well it had gone. The variable that still existed was how advanced Mom's Alzheimer's was and that none of us could predict how that would go. It all depended on Mom.

The next few days the conversations with the doctors on rotation were, for lack of a better way to put it, all over the place. In one breath they would communicate we needed to be prepared for Mom to not ever be able to leave the hospital as they thought it was a real possibility she wouldn't make it. Then the conversations turned to thinking about where we wanted her to go after she was discharged from the hospital. I realized the medical professionals couldn't always accurately communicate where we were with Mom, but it sure made for an emotional roller coaster attempting to navigate those conversations daily.

Dad and I knew this time we wouldn't be able to bring Mom home yet. The first time she had broken her hip, her cognitive ability was much stronger, and she was easier to direct and work with. Since she had experienced obvious declines since then, we knew that it would take a skilled nursing facility to address her current challenges if she had a chance of being able to walk again. We were provided with several options and thankfully were able to secure her a spot at what was classified as a five-star facility. Plans were made for transport, and we knew we had made the best decision based on the reality that currently existed.

I stayed with Mom to make sure she had a smooth transition from the hospital, and Dad left so he could be waiting on her when she arrived at the facility. Mom did well despite her current challenges, and I followed the ambulance to what would be her home for the time being. Mom got settled in, and at first glance, everything seemed pretty nice. Mom had a private room, bathroom, and closet. The room was tastefully decorated, and there was a TV to watch if she wanted to. I doubted she would watch it much, though, as it was difficult for her to follow any type of storyline these days. Additionally, she had a nice view from the large windows in the room. Leaving her that day after getting her settled in was one of the hardest things Dad and I would ever do. We both found that each time we came to visit her and then left, it never got any easier. We knew this really was our only option at the time, but it feels as if you're abandoning your loved one even though common sense tells you you're not.

This would be the first year since Mom and Dad had been married that she wouldn't be home for Christmas. We did our best to celebrate the day, but it just wasn't the same. We went out to spend time with Mom. They had had a small party at the facility, and Mom had received a Christmas shirt that she was wearing. The food they served was above average, and we had accepted this just was how Christmas was going to go this year.

In the midst of this, Dad and I had met with the two physical therapists that would be working with Mom to try to get her back on her feet again. I was told I needed to purchase a pair of tennis shoes for her as well as tops and pants because they would be getting her up on her feet. I immediately purchased the items they had requested and had them accessible in Mom's closet in just a couple of days. I was excited that they were ready to work with Mom and get her up and moving.

Dad and I both offered to help out with her physical therapy as we obviously knew her better than anyone else and could offer valuable

Chapter 8

insight into what could help facilitate the process of her walking again. While both of these therapists I found to be nice, I really felt like they didn't listen to what Dad and I had to say. They were both very loud with her. I don't mean to say they were mean, but they spoke to her as if she had a hearing problem. My Mom could hear even the slightest of noises, and I would watch her facial expressions as they spoke to her. I could almost read her mind as if she was thinking, "Don't they know I can hear?" I believe their approach made Mom hesitant and kept her from fully engaging in the sessions. When Dad tried to intervene, he was corrected. It was an extremely frustrating process, but Dad and I both kept our hopes up that everything they were doing with Mom would eventually "click" and she would be back to walking in no time at all.

During this time, she was back on her regular insurance, but one of her previous hospice caregivers came out every week to check on Mom and visit with her for a little bit. We would run into her occasionally when we had to come to visit Mom. If I had to point one thing out that made this difficult situation more bearable, it would be the genuine care and concern she received from the individuals from hospice. She didn't have to come out to see Mom, but she chose to, and that meant everything in the world to me and Dad. Anyone who was going to go above and beyond to be good to her was number one in our eyes.

As we had expected, her wrist with the pin became an ongoing issue during her recovery. She was fixated on it and would continually fiddle with it. I can't even begin to tell you how many times her wrist had to be rewrapped because she had completely undone it to get to the pin. Dad had a great idea that we could get a zip-up hooded sweatshirt and I could use hemming tape to close the end of the sleeve. It would be easy to get off of her quickly but would also protect the wrist and keep her from pulling the bandage off of it. I ordered the sweatshirt and fixed the sleeve. We took it out to the facility, and when we asked about putting it on her, we were told it would be a liability. Dad offered to sign any paperwork that would absolve them from any responsibility with this, but they didn't budge. We were told they would speak to upper management about the possibility, but in retrospect, they were just stalling us and really had no intention of following through with these conversations. How painfully evident at that point it became that we weren't even able to employ a common-sense approach to help my mom.

It was time for Mom to have a check-up on her wrist and hip. Unfortunately, the doctor did not choose to make visits to the facility she was in, so I was told she would be transported by ambulance to the doctor's office and I was to meet them in the waiting room. I was already there when they brought Mom in. She still wasn't far enough in her recovery to be transported in a wheelchair, so she came in on the gurney. She was in pain and extremely upset. She was drooling at the mouth and was very vocal. They actually expected her to be in the waiting room with all of the other patients waiting in this kind of shape. I tried to calm her as best as I could, but she only would say she was in pain and wanted to go home. I went to the front desk to inquire if there was a room in the back where she could be taken to wait on the doctor as this was creating an incredibly stressful situation. They were absolutely no help. Finally, she was called to the back after about an hour of this.

As professionally as I could, I let the doctor know that what my mom had endured in the waiting room was absolutely inhumane. She certainly deserved more privacy and respect than what was being given to her at that time. He did not argue and agreed with me. The plan moving forward would be she would have the first appointment in the morning or immediately after lunch to ensure she would never have to be subjected to this type of situation again. The next appointment was made. They decided to put a cast on her at this visit to avoid the continual issue of her unwrapping the bandage, and hopefully this would help with the fixation she had on the pin in her wrist. Guess what? Mom figured out a way to get the cast off too. You had to give her credit. She was a determined woman!

No sooner had I ordered and gotten Mom's tennis shoes, pants, and shirts in that the physical therapists made another request. They had decided Mom was not responding to their therapy as quickly as they hoped, and they made the decision she needed gowns instead. Not wanting Mom to go without whatever she needed, I quickly got together another order for several gowns for her. When I delivered them to the facility, they immediately cut them up the back so it would be easier to get them on and off of Mom. I knew they had many other patients that also required their attention, but it saddened me this was where we were at. I felt as if they were giving up on Mom. Dad and I both felt helpless.

What Dad and I knew would eventually happen finally happened. Mom got the wrap off of her wrist pushed the pin almost all the way into her arm. That was a fun call to receive from the facility. They told me they would need to transport her to the hospital to determine the next steps to address this current issue. I arrived at the hospital and was directed back to one of the ER rooms where Mom was waiting. She was in decent spirits, and we waited for the doctor to find out what could be done. It was a long day in the ER. Apparently, her doctor was in surgery and was receiving information from other doctors on staff and attempting to determine the best course of action moving forward.

They decided to x-ray Mom's wrist to see how well it was healing before making any decisions. Thankfully, they were able to bring the x-ray machine to her, which helped lessen her anxiety level. She obviously didn't know who I was but did recognize me as a familiar face, so I was able to provide some level of comfort for her in an otherwise stressful situation.

One of the doctors came back in and said that based on her x-rays, the wrist had healed enough to remove the pin. She communicated she would be able to do this without putting Mom under anesthesia. I asked if it was okay if I remained in the room to help distract her if needed while this was taking place, and she agreed it would be okay. Actually, I could sense relief in her voice as she said this was not a situation they were typically faced with, and I was glad to feel as if I would be able to provide some level of assistance.

When the doctor and her assistant came back to the room to perform the procedure, it was already after five o'clock in the evening. I suspected Mom had not had anything to eat during the day yet and made a mental note to make sure that was the first thing I addressed when she was transported back to the facility. Mom and I watched as the doctor began the process of removing the pin from Mom's wrist. She never whimpered, cried, flinched, or batted an eye. I had not realized how long the pin actually was until it was completely out of her wrist. I could understand now why Mom was so fixated on it continually; it would have bothered me too. Mom seemed relieved it was out, and we all bragged on her for what a great job she did, and she thanked us with a smile.

We would have to wait several more minutes before they were able to have anyone come pick her up to transport her back to the facility. I told her as soon as we got back, I would make sure she could get some dinner. The two EMTs who came to pick her up were so incredibly nice. They were in good spirits and seemed to genuinely enjoy their job. They both joked with Mom who joked right back at them. It was good to have some laughter after what had been a long and stressful day. They loaded her into the ambulance, and I told them I would meet them there.

I actually arrived back at the facility before them and was waiting in Mom's room for them. After they got Mom settled, I went to the nurse's station to inquire about Mom's dinner. They said they were currently delivering meals and hers should arrive at the room in no time at all. What had been a long day became even longer. She was such a trooper. I know by this time she was starving, and I was as well. We waited patiently, but no dinner arrived. I went back to the nurse's station to inquire once more and was told they must've already completed their rounds and would warm up something from the kitchen.

Finally, Mom's dinner arrived. You could tell it had been warmed up, and some of the food was a little tough. Mom had experienced difficulty in the hospital and in the nursing facility with being able to feed herself and chew up some food items, so I sat down beside her bed

Chapter 8

and proceeded to cut up her food and get her tea and water ready with straws. I took my time and fed her bite after bite until with a smile, she said, "that was good enough." No one ever came to check on her during this time, and I was frustrated with that, but maybe they were having difficulty with another patient. I tried to keep an open mind. I made sure Mom had the bedside table close enough to get water if she wanted it. I tucked her in, gave her a kiss, and told her goodnight. I exited her room, let the nurses station know I was on my way out, and walked out to my car. I realized I wasn't even hungry anymore. What a day it had been.

Chapter 9

In the midst of buying everything from shirts and pants to gowns, Mom's clothes were going missing. I guess I should have known I needed to put her name in all of her clothes, but with all of the back and forth of what they wanted her to have and then didn't want her to have, I guess I dropped the ball and didn't. I was able to go into the laundry room with the ladies and go through the racks of clothes until I was able to locate everything that belonged to Mom. Also, the jacket I had worked on so Mom wouldn't bother her wrapped wrist had magically disappeared. If they didn't want her to have it, they could have at least told us to take it home.

Physical therapy sessions continued but with no communication of real progress. I didn't really understand their approach but tried not to be critical as I reminded myself, I never appreciated when a parent had tried to tell me how do my job as an assistant school principal. Looking back though, I believe if they had just listened to Dad and me, she would've walked again, but as they say, that's "water under the bridge," so there's no sense reliving and belaboring the issue.

It was time again for a visit to Mom's doctor to check on her hip and wrist. I was told to meet Mom at the doctor's office as I had before, and that was all of the information I was provided with. I was waiting in the building, but Mom had still not shown up yet. About that time, I received a call on my phone that the van was there with Mom and wanted to know where I was. I told them that first, I did not agree to her being transported in a van as she still wasn't walking and that none of this information had been relayed to me. The longer Mom spent at this five-star facility, the more Dad I wondered how they had actually earned it considering the extremely ineffective communication we had experienced to this point.

I went down the stairs and apologized to the driver of the van as it wasn't his fault the facility hadn't provided me with the needed information. He gave me his card and told me to give him a call as soon as Mom was finished and he would be back to pick her to take her back to the facility. I thanked him and wheeled Mom to the waiting room. She was taken back quickly as agreed upon by the doctor at the last visit. When the nurses saw her, they assumed she would be able to get up out of the wheelchair on her own. This is where the fun began.

I let them know I had been blindsided that she had arrived by van and not by ambulance. I communicated she still was not able to walk and thought it was going to make this whole situation quite challenging with getting her on the x-ray table. They agreed and let me know my concerns were completely justifiable.

The medical staff worked together to determine a plan to get Mom out of the chair and onto the x-ray table. As soon as she was lifted out of the chair, it was evident she had not been changed or taken to the bathroom in quite some time. Urine splashed everywhere and was pooled in the bottom of the wheelchair seat. I wondered once again how this facility that came so highly recommended had earned a five-star rating. At that moment if I could've assigned them a negative number, I would've without giving it a second thought.

The medical staff worked together quickly and efficiently. They also made sure that Mom didn't suffer any further embarrassment with the situation. They also problem-solved until they found her some dry clothes since the clothes she had been wearing were obviously soaked through. One of the head nurses stepped out to call the facility and I was told she as professionally as she could "gave them a piece of her mind." They were told never to send a patient to them again without the necessary means of transportation. Thankfully, the x-ray showed that Mom's hip was healing as they had hoped. She still had not taken any steps, though.

Chapter 9

As they were finishing up with her, I called Dad, and before I could even ask, he let me know he would meet me at the facility and whoever got there first would request to meet with the head of the facility. We both were on the same page that what Mom had just went through should have never happened and they were out of line as well as negligent with how they had handled her care and transport.

One of the nurses wheeled Mom out to me, and I expressed how thankful I was for each of them that had assisted with her that afternoon. She said with a smile, "That's what we're here for." I know in my heart, though, when people go above and beyond what their job requires. I had witnessed it that day with my own eyes. It was a comfort to know there were still individuals that cared that much about their chosen profession. It's moments like those that provided hope in what seemed like a hopeless situation more days than not.

I called the driver to come pick up Mom. She and I chatted while we sat in the downstairs lobby waiting for her ride. The one good thing about her disease was she had already forgotten what had just transpired at her office visit. It wasn't too long before the driver arrived, and I waited until I was sure she was loaded into the van and settled. I thanked the driver and walked to my car, wondering what excuses we would encounter when Dad and I spoke with the staff at the facility.

Dad was already there when I arrived. I did not inquire how fast he had driven, but I imagine it most definitely exceeded the posted limit. The head of the facility wasn't available, so we were greeted by the assistant of the facility. The one thing we could all agree on was that the communication that had occurred to this point with us had been absolutely atrocious. Dad and I both voiced all of the concerns we had experienced since Mom had been admitted to the facility. We also made it clear we had attempted to follow the chain of command regarding our concerns but were confident that nothing we inquired about or commented on was ever passed on to others. We were both provided with business cards with the head assistant's direct extension as well as inundated with promises for better care and communication from this point forward as they were of course a five-star facility.

Dad and I made plans to split our visits when we could to try to be more effective in ensuring Mom was receiving the care she required consistently. Her best friend and sister were also on board and would let Dad and me know if they witnessed anything of concern when they were visiting her.

Dad and I had both noticed that Mom was still having difficulty with eating. When stopping by to visit, it was breakfast time. If possible, they liked to wheel the patients down to the dining area to eat. I imagine it was partly due to staffing issues, expecting one to two people to have eyes on many. So, when we arrived at Mom's room, we figured she had been taken to the dining area. When we sat down with her, we noticed she had not touched her food. We both worked with her and "jump-started" her eating I guess you could say. In that moment, we realized that she still needed a lot of prompting. When we shared our concerns, we were told that she could join a group in the back from that point forward where there were more personnel who could assist with this. To my knowledge, this never occurred.

Their answer was to send in a professional who could show us that Mom just needed more finger foods and then she could eat on her own. I watched her work with Mom and knew this wasn't the answer, but as with everything else, Dad and I always tried to meet them halfway and agreed to see if the new menu selections would work. After this, they wanted to know if it would be okay to wheel Mom down to the dining area where they were going to play some games. Dad and I agreed and went down with her to help get her settled.

The game that had been chosen was Bingo. Cards and markers were handed out to all of the patients seated at the tables. Mom looked bewildered when she was handed hers, so Dad and I helped get her set up. We both joked with Mom and the other ladies sitting at the table and got prepared for numbers to be called.

I know I shouldn't have been taken unaware or shocked in the least, but I was. I realized as each number was called that Mom couldn't listen to the number and determine whether or not it was located on her playing card. Dad realized the same thing about another lady sitting at the table, so he was helping her as well. Looking around, I noticed there were quite a few patients struggling with finding numbers too. How incredibly sad we were at the point that Mom couldn't engage in a game of Bingo, but that was where we were and as difficult as it was, we were just going to have to find a way to accept it.

After a few rounds of play, the cards and markers were collected. The nurse announced it was now snack time and she would be around to see what kind of ice cream each patient would like. Mom brightened up a bit when hearing this and I was relieved since we had just powered through the lackluster game of Bingo. When the nurse got to Mom, she asked her if she would like chocolate, strawberry, or vanilla. Mom looked at me and said, "What do I want"? I told her I'd go with chocolate, so chocolate it was. She ate every bite; it was easy to get her started with the spoon and she seemed like she thoroughly enjoyed it. Once she finished, Dad and I let her know we would be on our way but would be back soon to see her. It never got any easier to leave her during her entire stay there. It was as if your heart was being ripped out over and over again, but hopefully she would be up on her feet again and we could get her home.

Mom was wearing mainly gowns at this point. The tennis shoes had never been placed on her feet. One Friday afternoon as I was wrapping up things at work, I received a call from one of the physical therapists. She stated that Mom was just not responding to the plan they had in place for her, and Dad and I needed to start thinking what next steps would be. I pushed back a little bit as Dad and I had both offered to help and weren't taken up on our requests. We were only grudgingly included if we were already there when they came to work with her. By the time we got off of the phone, we had a date and time agreed upon when Dad and I could come assist. She also said we would be given a two-week window before we would have to decide next steps for Mom if she continued not to respond to the therapy.

Chapter 10

Before the scheduled physical therapy session, Dad had gone out to spend time with Mom one day when I was still at work. He was told by the staff that Mom had actually stood on her feet that day! Finally, she was making some progress, no matter how small. Dad called to let me know, and we both felt better than we had in quite a while. Hopefully this was the beginning of her being able to walk again. Maybe things were looking up!

The day of the physical therapy session arrived, and I had gotten approval to leave work for the session and return when it concluded. Dad was already in the room when I got there. The two physical therapists arrived, and the session began. I was so excited and just knew this would be the day that Mom would be able to take a few steps. Dad was cautiously optimistic, but I know he was thinking the same thing too. It was not to happen that day. Mom just couldn't do it. The therapists felt her cognitive ability was so far declined that she really couldn't follow their directions and engage in the therapy to the level to produce any kind of consistent results. I imagined I would be getting a call from the physical therapists in the next few days, and that's exactly what happened.

One of the therapists reached out late one Friday afternoon and said what I already knew was coming, but instead of the original communication of a two-week window to make arrangements, it was now Dad and I needed to have a plan in place by the following Tuesday. I pushed back once again and reminded her of our previous communication. She relented, and I called Dad to let him to know we would need to make some tough decisions pretty quickly. I had been given the contact information for a representative with a home health care company, so I quickly made an appointment on a day when Dad and I could both meet with her. The representative had responded quickly. She would meet us in Mom's room the following week to meet her, to evaluate her needs, and to discuss services they provided so Dad and I could make an informed decision.

The following week, Dad and I arrived and were waiting in Mom's room when the representative arrived. She completed her evaluation, and then Mom was taken down to the dining hall for scheduled activities. She shared with us all of the services offered and the different levels of service as far as hours that could be purchased. She also asked if Dad had been in the military. He had served in the Army with an honorable discharge, so she let him know that he could receive benefits as a veteran that could assist with paying for these services. She gave us the name of a contact at the local veteran's office in town and felt confident they could assist. We told her we would check on the potential benefits and would be back in touch with which of the plans she presented that we thought would work best for Mom.

We arrived at the local veteran's office and waited patiently as they finished up with another client before welcoming us into the office. When we entered the office, we explained the purpose for our visit. The woman was nice but made it clear that we shouldn't count on securing any benefits for assisting with my mom's care. She stated that Dad had served during a time of peace. If he had served during wartime, he would've had a better chance of receiving benefits, but it was still no guarantee. As there was really nothing left to say, we thanked her for her time and left the office.

When Dad and I got back to his truck and got in, we just sat there for a minute. We felt like we'd been sent on a wild goose chase and had obviously returned empty-handed. It was as if we had been misled by the home health care representative who said she "knew them so well" at the veteran's office and was "sure we could get some assistance." At this point though, we really had no other option than to continue to work with her and see what we could get in place for Mom. The clock was ticking.

Chapter 10

After several conversations and lots of questions, Dad and I made what we thought would be the best decision for Mom. We had already spoken to a representative from hospice, and they were ready to start back with Mom's services at home. They quickly went to work on delivering a hospital bed as well as a lift so we could transport her from the wheelchair to the bed and vice versa. We also scheduled home health care for a couple of days a week so they could assist based on the list of services that were communicated to us.

Plans were made to transport Mom home. Of course, even though she still wasn't walking, insurance once again stated that ambulance transport wasn't "medically necessary," so you do what you have to in those types of situations, and we paid for the transport. We were just glad that she was coming home. We were both confident that we would be able to have Mom up and moving again.

Since Mom was coming home, I knew even with hospice care and the possibility of additional assistance from home health that it would still be an enormous change and challenge. I made the decision to take a family medical leave from my job. I had been an educator for almost twenty-seven years, and the majority of that time was spent in an elementary school just minutes from my house. I currently was serving as the assistant principal, and it was an incredibly difficult decision to make. I knew, though, that Dad and Mom both needed me and because I had worked diligently all of those years, I had more than enough days to take as needed. Looking back, I am so thankful I made the decision I did, and I have not regretted it for one moment. The time spent with her was priceless.

Chapter 11

The first day of home health services came, and Dad and I both waited on the sitter to arrive. We were told that some of the services their employee could provide were to fix Mom meals, change her, and supervise her as needed. I agreed to walk the employee through more specifically what those services would like for Mom, and then we could go from there. The time for the sitter to arrive came and went. I called the service to inquire, and they stated their employee had been delayed but she would be there soon.

Once she arrived, I began instructing her on what Dad and I expected and what kind of routine we were trying to put in place for Mom. She was very sweet but seemed a little unsure of herself, which I would think would be completely normal coming into a stranger's house to help with their loved one. I took her back to Mom's room and let her get acquainted with Mom as I fed Mom her breakfast. Afterward, I asked her to help me change Mom so she could see the system I had worked out. Then, I left her to sit with Mom while I went to the living room to talk with Dad.

We both decided that even with that morning's mix-up, this arrangement might work out. We had hospice scheduled to come out on the days that home health care wasn't coming, so we guessed we should give it a try.

Before the sitter left for the day, we asked her how she felt about taking care of Mom and if the days we needed her would work out. She agreed and she contacted her boss, and I contacted the service as well so everyone would be on the same page, but unfortunately, that did not occur.

Once again, Dad and I found ourselves waiting for the sitter. When I called the service, they stated there had been a miscommunication and they had not entered the days correctly in the system. I told them the sitter had been wonderful but the inconsistency with how they addressed scheduling was unacceptable. I told them Dad and I would not be needing anything further from them as we needed a service we could rely on. A few days later, I received a call from one of the supervisors. At first, she started out by telling me Dad would not receive his deposit back. I kept my cool and told her she might want to hear everything that we had been though first.

As I relayed the events of the previous couple of weeks leading up to where we were now with a discontinuation of services, she paused and then did something I did not expect . . . apologized. Dad and I had consistently been complimentary of the sitter and had made it clear it was not her that we had the problem with. As the conversation continued, the supervisor went on to tell me the representative Dad and I had dealt with from the start had been let go. She said there had been evidence she had misled families during the intake process and it had caused multiple issues. Dad and I could certainly attest to that! When the call was complete, the supervisor and I were both on good terms, and Dad's deposit would be returned. I wished the supervisor well on her endeavor to get things straightened out for future clients. I certainly didn't want any other families to experience what Dad and I had. We were trying to do everything we could to keep the focus on Mom and what she needed.

It took a couple of days for reality to set in regarding the tremendous responsibility Dad and I had just taken on with declining any further services from home health. Now it was just us and hospice.

Mom had increasingly declined over the last several weeks. Her agitation had become a concern as she was attempting repeatedly to pull sheets off her bed and try to swing her legs out to exit the bed, even though it had been several months since she had been able to walk. Dad and I had resorted to "tucking her in" as you would a small child who you didn't want to fall out of the bed. We would have to repeat this multiple times throughout the day and night to ensure her safety. It was confusing to her when we did this, and it broke our hearts to have to resort to this, but we knew the main goal was keeping her safe.

One evening after changing her and tucking her in after what seemed like the millionth time, I gave her a kiss and told her I loved her and prepared to leave for the evening. It had become a routine I knew well. I was told I would never be able to change her myself but had become quite the master of the task. Please understand, it did not start out this way. One of the first times I changed her by myself, Mom decided she was having no part of it. In frustration, I threw down the wipes on her bed, and before I could even get around to the other side of the bed, Dad appeared in the room. He had set up a video camera in her room so he could monitor her when he was in the living room. At this moment, he had a "heart to heart" discussion with me, and from that day forward I never lost my temper with her again. It's difficult to accept when roles change, and at that moment it really hit home that I had now become the parent and she was the child. I prayed I could have half the patience with her as she did with me when I was growing up.

When going through her things, I found a story she had written about me that shows how wonderful my mom was and how much patience she had with me.

God's In His Heaven

Obviously, God knew what he was doing when he created children, especially babies. Most of the time, they are sweet, cute, and adorable. They do have their moments, however . . . We waited eight long years for our own bundle of joy to arrive, and there were many, many days when I had to pinch myself to be sure I wasn't dreaming. From the moment you were placed in my arms, I experienced a feeling of euphoria that I couldn't exactly put into words, but I devoutly hoped it would never go away. I knew that nothing else in this world would ever equal that feeling, and I told God so, too. I'll bet He grinned at that. Hey, there's no reason to believe that God doesn't grin at us sometimes. He probably shook his head and thought to himself, "Wait, just wait..."

Well, we finally made it through bathtime, tooth-brushing, and "Now I lay me down to sleep/bless everybody in the universe..." Let me tell you, I just couldn't wait for lights out. Then that small, still voice of my conscience decreed, however, that it would be unfair to toss her in with her doll and stuffed animals without our usual bedtime reading session. So I grabbed a book and prepared to zoom through it. Obviously, I was not angling for Parent of the Year at that point.

She settled down to listen, no doubt as worn out from the friction of the day as I was. I made it through Jack and the Beanstalk in record time. No speed reader on Earth could have read that story more quickly. I bent over to give her a half-hearted kiss and reached for the light switch all in one rapid motion. Just as I was about to make my grand escape, I heard this little voice softly saying, "Would you read just one poem, please, Mom?" I reached reluctantly for a book of poems. I snapped it open at random, and the following words seemed to leap off of the page at me:

> "God's in His Heaven,
> All's right with the world."

All of my anger and frustration melted away... and I saw Beth's small body relax and I began to read quietly, softly... I read poem after poem. I don't know exactly when my daughter fell asleep, but I continued to read, letting the words of long-dead poets seep into my soul.

Finally, I laid the book aside, adjusted the covers and lightly kissed my daughter. I slept well that night. So did Beth.

My thoughts go back to that night whenever life seems too much for me. Then I close my eyes, picture my four-year old asking for a poem ("just one Mom, please") and I let those words work their soothing magic once more... God's in His Heaven. All's right with the world. Thank you, Robert Browning.

When leaving that evening, I stopped to look at the video to check in one last time. Dad and I had worked out a schedule where I would

Chapter 11

arrive between 6:00 and 7:00 a.m. in the morning and would leave around 4:00–6:00 p.m. depending on how her day had gone. He would handle the night shift and typically would sleep on the daybed I bought to place in her room so we could stay close to her. As I was watching the camera screen, I noticed bright balls of light in her room. Some would move slowly, others would move quickly, and some would blink as if they had a pulse. Being a fan of anything paranormal, I immediately recognized what these balls of light were: "orbs." I called Dad over to share what I was seeing and explain what they were. I had seen them on TV shows, but never had I witnessed them in real life. We both stared at the screen in pure amazement of what we were seeing. How could this be? After some time, we began to try to "debunk" the balls of light, but there was no plausible explanation for what we were seeing. This moment signified the beginning of the end for Mom. It also began a period of time for me and Dad that we will never forget, nor will we ever take for granted. My Mom had one last task . . . one last mission and she taught it to me and Dad in such a way that we will both treasure this lesson until our time here on Earth is done.

Chapter 12

The next morning, I arrived at my usual time. I had experienced some difficulty sleeping the night before. Every time I thought I had settled enough to get some sleep, my mind reverted back to the images of the orbs Dad and I had witnessed on the video screen. At this point, part of me was questioning if we had actually seen them and another part of me was hoping I would be able to see them again. I wondered what the purpose and significance of the orbs were. We had been in a holding pattern with Mom as far as her dementia progression, so this new development brought more questions than answers.

Evening came, and I went through my routine as usual with Mom prior to leaving. I tucked her in and headed to the living room in anxious anticipation of what would be visible on the video camera. As Dad and I watched, we once again witnessed the orbs. I sat there mesmerized as I watched them float, zoom, pulsate, and dart all over her room. At times, the orbs came so quickly toward the camera that it reminded me of being in the James K. Polk cinema as a four-year-old watching Star Wars and seeing the Millenium Falcon zooming through space. Dad asked me what my thoughts were regarding recording her as she slept to see if we could determine any type of pattern related to the orbs. I agreed it would be a good idea and maybe we could gain some additional insight into understanding what was occurring.

Arriving the next day, I traded out with Dad and dozed off until I heard Mom begin to stir. As I looked up from the daybed, I saw her leaning over the rail of the hospital bed and smiling. She said, "There you are!" In the moment you can never understand how much you'll miss words like these later. Of course, she didn't know my name, but I was at least viewed as a familiar, kind, and safe individual. As I sat up on the side of the daybed, she let me know that her mother was there in the room. When I asked where she was, she said, "sitting beside of you." I hesitated for a moment and then asked her to say hello to my grandmother and to let her know I missed her. She smiled and said she would be happy to do so. Dad had gotten up by this time, and I followed him out to the living room to let him know what Mom had said. Hospice was due to come out that morning, and we both agreed we should communicate this recent development to them.

Based on Mom "seeing" her mother, hospice determined it was time to increase her weekly visits. They said it was typical toward the end of life for patients to begin seeing those who had already crossed over. It was hard to accept, but Dad and I both knew there was no miraculous recovery that was going to occur at this point, and it was important to us that Mom was as comfortable as possible. So if this was the next step, then we would embrace it and handle it to the best of our ability.

After hospice left that morning, Dad asked if I'd like to watch the video to see what happened overnight with Mom and the orbs. He mentioned some specific time frames that I might want to start with where he noted Mom had become somewhat agitated. I inserted the SD card in my computer and searched for the times he had given me. As I watched the minutes/seconds tick away on the video, it was unbelievable how accurately he had conveyed the times to me. Every time I searched, orbs became visible on the video. Not only that, these balls of light also seemed to be attempting to interact with Mom. As orbs flew toward her, you could see her look their way or respond by pulling the blanket up over her head. I showed Dad what I had found. We were both at a loss as to how we could help her navigate what was happening to her.

Amid navigating the last stage of Mom's Alzheimer's, I was also trying to continue with other life developments, such as my son getting engaged. That Saturday we were scheduled to tour a potential wedding venue with my son, his fiancé, and her parents. We had a wonderful time, and her parents ended up securing the venue that day. I had ridden with my son and his fiancé, and we were headed back to my parents'

Chapter 12

house when I received a call from Dad. He said Mom had experienced an episode and to come back as soon as we could.

When we arrived, I went straight back to Mom's room where Dad was sitting with her. She was slowly coming out of whatever medical event had occurred and was becoming more lucid. I sat down with her and held her hand. She turned her head to me and very clearly and without any hesitation said to me, "God said be prepared!" Little did I know at that time how prepared I would need to be in the coming weeks and months. Looking back, I can now see and feel God's immense love remembering that moment.

Dad and I decided to reach out to the hospice nurse on call to see if there was anything we could do for Mom. When she came out that evening, after examining her, she commented it could have been several things that had happened, but there really wasn't anything we could do as she was experiencing another decline. To this day, Dad and I believe Mom suffered a cardiac event that day, and at this point, only a couple of weeks were left for Mom here on Earth. She was coming closer to leaving us for her heavenly home. Neither myself nor my dad could have prepared ourselves for what we would experience in those last moments.

The days ticked away one by one. Hospice visits had increased, and the nurse was coming out every other day now. A representative from hospice had also stopped by to provide us with literature on the end-of-life stage and see if we had any questions. We couldn't have asked for any nicer individuals that assisted us through this process. All the hospice employees who came out to take care of Mom were genuinely caring and thoughtful. Dad and I never felt as if they rushed through the motions of taking care of her or discounted any of the many questions we asked. We could not have taken care of her at home without their help.

On this particular morning, the nurse sat down with me to go over Mom's medical readings. She shared with me that the numbers were slowly deteriorating and it was time to consider starting her on morphine. I had read enough to know we were preparing for what most likely would be her final days. Dad and I knew this was what would keep Mom most comfortable and agreed to start the morphine.

I was given a medical lesson on administration of the morphine and how to increase as needed based on observing Mom. I guess I had a look on my face. I've been told I do not possess a "poker face." The nurse reassured me not to worry that she was certain I could not overdose Mom. I smiled with relief as she had so quickly ascertained my worries and concerns.

During these days, Dad and I continued to observe and record the orbs. They were becoming brighter and more numerous now. The orbs continued to defy any explanation of how they moved and the various times they would become visible throughout the evening. These continued observations brought up something that Dad and I needed to discuss and agree on as the end was drawing near. Do we record her as she's passing? This was not a decision we made lightly. We both decided this was something we needed and wanted to do. We had no idea what we would observe, if anything. We would both end up being amazed at what we witnessed, and it would forever change how we both viewed what happens when a person dies.

When I sat down with the nurse that Friday, she discussed that Mom's numbers had already taken another downward turn. After updating Dad with this latest news, I contacted our family members to let them know if they'd like to come spend some time with her, it would be best if they would come on over as Mom was rapidly declining. My aunt and my mother's best friend made plans to come spend the next day with her. That evening when I went to go through my normal routine with Mom, I couldn't bear to turn her like she would have to go through in order to change her. She had already gotten to the point of refusing any liquids and food, so I knew she was not in dire need of changing. Dad and I agreed it was best not to disturb her.

Chapter 13

When I arrived the next morning, a subtle rattle in her breathing was already becoming noticeable. I made myself comfortable in my usual spot on the daybed in her room. My aunt and my Mom's best friend arrived soon after. We spent the day taking turns sitting with her and listening to her as the rattle became increasingly louder throughout the day. I have read this is not painful to the person, but if you've ever been with someone who has had this, it's got to be one of the most helpless feelings in the world to not be able to intervene other than administering morphine.

By that evening, everyone was worn out, and there of course was no way of knowing how much longer Mom would be in this state. Dad and I assured her sister and friend we would contact them when anything changed and encouraged them to go home and try to get some rest.

Dad and I discussed it, and it was decided I would go ahead and stay the night and continue to administer the morphine as needed. He went out to the living room to try to take a nap in his recliner. He also started recording the video as we had both earlier agreed. I turned the lights off in her room and sat down on the daybed. Her breathing (death rattle) continued, and I prayed to God for peace and comfort for her.

It had been about an hour when I heard the gasp. I immediately jumped up and went to her side. At that time, Dad came through the door, turned on the light, and joined on the other side of her bed. He had been asleep in the recliner, and something had told him to get up. We both were there with her as she took her last breath. The unrelenting road she had traveled with Alzheimer's had finally come to an end. It had truly been a long goodbye, and now she was gone.

I stood there in disbelief and grief, gently brushing her hair with my hand. How did time fly by so quickly? She has served in so many important roles throughout her life: daughter, sister, wife, mother, employee, volunteer, writer, and friend, to name a few. Now it had all ended in what seemed like a blink of an eye.

Dad called hospice as he knew I was in no state to make the call. He stoically communicated that his wife had passed, although I heard the quaver in his voice that probably only I could have detected.

We waited for the hospice worker to arrive. When she did, she was one of the nicest people I have had the pleasure of meeting. She worked quickly to clean up Mom before the funeral home personnel arrived. She made conversation that kept me from falling apart but was not so verbose as to cause angst. We worked together through unavoidable tasks such as accounting for and discarding medications.

As she concluded her tasks, the funeral personnel arrived. She would be transported to the funeral home and cremated per her wishes. I will never forget watching them take her out the front door and down the steps away from the home she had lived in for forty-nine years. I was grateful Dad and I had been able to bring her home from the assisted living facility, even though it was one of the most challenging times of our lives.

I watched as the taillights of the hearse disappeared into the night, and I walked back into the house. Dad and I talked for a few minutes. At this point, everything was a blur, so I don't even recall exactly what we talked about. I imagine it was probably plans for the following Monday to go to the funeral home to finalize her obituary and complete any required paperwork. Earlier in the day, my son had come by to borrow my car because his truck was in the shop for repairs. If life teaches you anything, it's that regardless of circumstances, other life situations will come up and must be addressed. Maybe they're meant to be distractions from your current situation, but I could have done without that distraction.

Chapter 13

Dad offered to drive me home as I only live a couple of miles down the road. I had another idea though. In the garage was my mom's car, a 1993 Oldsmobile Regency, and I wanted to drive it home. He got me the keys and even backed it out of the garage for me, so I would be ready to head down the driveway. In the CD player was a John Denver CD. I don't even remember the song that was playing as I made my way home, but it didn't matter because I was in her car, listening to her music, and it made me feel close to her. Saturday, March 9, 2024 was Mom's last day on this Earth, but what happens after? In a few days, Dad and I would have indisputable evidence of what happens when passing and would find a peace we both desperately needed.

Monday morning arrived, and Dad and I made our way to the funeral home to finalize plans. We were joined by my son, my mom's sister, and her husband. Of course, it was a stressful day. You think you've thought of everything to make the process easier, but in actuality, I don't think that exists. Yes, her arrangements had been pre-planned, but what did we forget? Her photo for the obituary. My son assured his grandad he could open the safe, retrieve the photo, and be back in no time at all. Unfortunately, it didn't work out that way. Somehow, he messed up the combination, and even my Dad couldn't get it to open. We ended up going with a picture I had of her in my photos on my phone when her engagement was announced, which worked perfectly. Why do we sometimes find ways to overcomplicate things that should be so easy?

We also had the task of determining what to do with her ashes. Originally, my Dad and I had thought we would spread her ashes on the farm where they had lived for almost fifty years, but as we were completing the paperwork, it just didn't seem right somehow. We decided to secure a spot in the mausoleum for her, and Dad would also be able to have his ashes with her when that day arrives. We both decided we wanted something more permanent for her where she wouldn't be forgotten. We both felt peace with making this decision and felt like it would help us both to move forward.

We all decided to head back to Mom and Dad's house, and my son offered to pick up some lunch. We still had the issue of the safe that would now not open. Dad looked through files as my mom was extremely organized and made sure everything was easily found and accessible. No luck. We even tried to call customer support, but no support was available, just a promise of how many more minutes until a customer service representative would assist that seemed to get longer rather than shorter. I then had a thought. I vaguely remembered something about when they bought the safe and something Mom had done to ensure only they could access it. I went back to the files my Dad had gone through, and under a different tab, there it was! She knew it would be too easy to file it under its actual name. Needless to say, there was a huge sense of relief felt by Dad. Mom was gone, but she was still solving problems. Why would we expect anything else? She was pretty awesome like that.

Chapter 14

The next day was Tuesday, and I went over to the house to help Dad with some paperwork. After concluding the tasks we needed to accomplish, he asked if I was ready to view the video from when Mom passed. I said I was ready, and he went to get the SD card as I powered on my laptop. I sat there watching, knowing what was to come next but still in a way wishing that somehow something would change but realizing it would not. I sat watching myself jump up from the daybed as I rushed to her side and saw Dad entering the door joining on the other side. In that last moment, as Dad and I stood by her, she took her last breath, and clearly visible on the video, a bright orb exited her body and flew up toward the ceiling until it was no longer in view. Mom had gone home.

Even reliving the moment that had made us so heartbroken, we felt a sense of immense relief and joy. We had witnessed with our own eyes this was not the end. When you take your last breath on this Earth, your journey is not over. She had gone home to be with God. All the questions we had mulled over, all the hesitation, all the doubt . . . gone. God loves us and He exists! We had been a part of something so much greater than the two of us. God had given Mom this one last mission in her earthly body, and she had accomplished it. The peace we both felt was indescribable. A heavenly home awaits.

Mom's story doesn't end here though . . .

A few days later, Mom's words still echoed in my mind: " God said be prepared!" You know how you sometimes have that feeling in the pit of your stomach that more is to come? That is exactly the feeling I was experiencing but had no idea what that would look like, sound like, or feel like. I was about to find out.

It was the morning of March 22nd. Mom had passed away on March 9th, and I had been back to work for almost a week. I received a text from my husband that the assisted living facility where his mother resided had told him to come immediately as his mother was in a rapid decline. His mother also was battling Alzheimer's as my mom had been.

I left work and a drive that should've taken thirty minutes ended up being more like an hour. When I arrived at the assisted living facility, my husband met me outside, and we headed to her room. I could hear his mother's labored breathing even before I made it through her doorway. They had just begun administering morphine earlier that morning, and his mother appeared unaware of anything going on around her. My husband was obviously having an extremely difficult time, and I took a seat beside the foot of her bed.

His brother had been there briefly before I arrived. The medical personnel had communicated she could pass anytime but could potentially make it until Sunday, so he decided to go ahead and leave. I was glad I was there for my husband, and even though his mother's passing would differ from that of my own mother, I had just been through it and somewhat knew what to expect.

His mother's breathing was nothing like my mother's. My mother had the "death rattle" that persisted and worsened throughout the day, but his mother's breathing was nothing like I had experienced. The time between her breaths would gradually increase. I found myself starting to count. As I watched her, I was able to determine from my own recent experience with my own mother when to request additional morphine from the medical staff. I let my husband know that my instinct was telling me his mother would not make it through the day.

As the minutes ticked on throughout the morning, medical personnel came in and out. They were wonderful and so caring with her. She had been verbal up until just a couple of days prior, and I believe even though they obviously did this for a living, there was still a sense of shock in how quickly his mother's health had deteriorated. I imagine no matter how many times you experience death, it's still traumatic as

Chapter 14

there's no textbook example to count on each time because there are so many variables.

I observed the time between her breaths was becoming more extended, and I focused on counting as a way to prepare myself and to be strong enough to help Jim navigate losing his mother. I remember getting to forty and hearing one last gasp, knowing she would not take another breath. The room radiated with a beautiful light, and she was finally at peace. Amazingly as I sent my husband to go get one of the medical personnel, they appeared at the door as if God had sent a message to "go check on her."

We watched as they confirmed she had passed. We then waited until contact was made with the funeral home to come and pick her up as well as make plans to deal with her belongings. My husband wanted as much as possible donated to the other patients in the facility as some of them would come in without very many belongings. We then left to come home.

Some might say how emotionally taxing it must've been for me to have just lost my own mother and then to have to endure losing my mother-in-law. I would be lying if I said it wasn't. I do look at it as I had been told by my mother that "God said be prepared." By experiencing her passing, I was able to be there for my husband and perhaps provide support I otherwise would not have been able to provide if I had not just been through the same thing myself.

I thought surely this was what my mother had referenced and now I could start the healing process and help my husband with his as well, but more was to come, so much more.

Chapter 15

It was Wednesday, May 8th. The day started out normal and uneventful. There was a weather forecast looming with the potential for hazardous weather, but I wasn't really worried. I had been down this road many times, and nothing bad had ever happened before. Maybe a blown off window shutter or a few tree limbs here and there, but nothing to cause fear or concern. I had no plans for taking any extreme measures to prepare and figured it would be like every other storm and turn out to be nothing more than a thunderstorm, some strong wind, and maybe a few lightning strikes. I couldn't have been more wrong.

I got in my car to leave my dad's house, and on my Apple Car Play, a religious song popped up that I had never searched for, nor did I recognize the Christian music artist. The intro of the song caught my attention, and so I left it to finish playing. I live close to my Dad, so the ride home was basically long enough for the song to play to the end. I really liked it, and after getting my dog Scout to take out in the backyard, I brought the speaker out and proceeded to listen to some of the other songs on the album. The wind was beginning to pick up a little, and Jim was almost home so I went back in the house with Scout. I felt a certain sense of peace and had very much enjoyed listening to the Christian artist. It had been a nice afternoon.

Once Jim was home, the weather deteriorated rapidly. Before I knew it, I was in the bathtub with my dog and my son on the phone and yelling at Jim to quit running to look out the window. He finally appeased me, and I could only pray that whatever was happening outside would be over soon and we would be safe. Once it was safe to come out, I walked out the back door of my house. The best way to describe what

I was met with was what I imagined a war zone would look like in my yard.

I saw my neighbor exiting her house, and she came over and hugged me, and I cried like a baby. The realization of what we had just lived through was hitting home fast. Mature trees had been uprooted as if someone had just pushed them over, and huge root systems were exposed. None of the trees in my yard survived the storm other than the two Bradford trees by the driveway. Trees in the front, back, and side yards were uprooted. Now think about what I'm saying: trees on all sides of my house were down. Other than one window shutter, the house was untouched. The insurance adjuster would confirm the garage door was bowed in a bit, but basically the confirmed EF3 tornado had stopped at the garage door and gone around the sides of the house.

When my dad pulled into the part of the driveway he could get to, even I could tell he was somewhat at a loss for words. When he spoke, he said, "Your mother was watching over you wasn't she?" She absolutely was. I am confident none of the events of that afternoon just happened. I know the religious song playing in my car when I started it that afternoon as well as my desire to listen to other songs on the album were no accident. The prayers I prayed that afternoon all were answered as I sat in a bathtub not knowing what was to come next. I know God protected my family and home that afternoon, and I will never take for granted what a blessing that was.

In the next days, I witnessed my neighborhood pull together to help one another. I'm not social by nature, but I forced myself to venture out to help others where I could, provide rides to the tornado relief hub, and just be a listening ear. Others were not as fortunate as I was, and by the time the tornado reached the end of my road, one of the houses was damaged so severely it was unlivable. Thankfully no lives were lost in my neighborhood, but the tornado did end up taking the life of one person.

It took a couple of months to clear trees and debris from our neighborhood. There are still areas such as waterways that need cleaning that are a constant reminder of that day. The area looks almost

Chapter 15

unrecognizable compared to what it originally looked like, but buildings can be repaired, and trees can be planted and grow. I think I can speak for everyone in saying we all realized how much worse it could've been, and I'm confident in saying God took care of us that day.

I believe Mom was looking out for me that day from heaven and protected me and my family. You could not convince me otherwise. I thought to myself . . . okay, "God said be prepared," and now I can get back to everyday life. Unfortunately, that was not the case. I would still have one more difficult life experience to live through, but it would also provide me with hope.

Chapter 16

Life was beginning to get back on track after the tornado. Days were back to their predictable tasks to accomplish, and summer was in full swing. There was one other thing though. My mom's younger brother by a couple of years had just been placed in hospice care. My uncle had lived on his own in their childhood home. His son had been trying to convince him to move in with him and his wife after breaking his arm. He was always fiercely independent but finally relented, and plans were made for the move.

His son and his wife are devout Catholics and attend mass diligently. My Uncle, though, was an atheist. I would venture to say his time in Vietnam in the war probably had a lot to do with this. We never had that conversation, but after reading about his time there as recorded by my mom, I can say I don't know how a person lives through an experience like that and comes out sane. The things he endured, no one should have to deal with under any circumstance.

So now he was in hospice, and needless to say, family members kept in the back of their mind that my uncle believed there was nothing after this life. That God doesn't exist. Of course, no one tried to push their belief on him but made themselves available if he wanted to talk.

It was of concern to me, but I knew I couldn't make him feel or believe the way I wanted him to. This is the uncle who taught me how to play tennis, genuinely expressed interest in whatever was going on in my life at the time, and had a sense of humor and wittiness that could rival the best. I was able to visit with him after Mom passed, and we had a really good conversation. I don't recall exactly everything we spoke about, but I remember it being comforting.

About two weeks before he passed, I went over to visit with him again. It was very hard to hear him with the weakness in his voice, but we chatted until he got tired. I prayed that somehow, someway, he would find his way to God so he could have a heavenly welcome. My cousin let me know after that he had a dream about my mom (his sister). He did not tell him everything from the dream but only that my mom was in a good place and he was at peace. I truly believe my mom talked to him about heaven and God. I believe in that moment, my uncle accepted Jesus Christ and was saved. I think there was a reason my mom preceded him in death. I think because of life experiences, this was the only way that he was able to be reached.

Not long after this, my uncle passed, and I am assured he went to his heavenly home. I am confident he joined my mom along with a multitude of other family members and is finally free from the burdens this world placed upon him. I can't even imagine what a joyous welcoming that was!

Conclusion

My dad and I hope that within the pages, you were able to find something that speaks to you regarding whatever you may currently be dealing with in your own walk in life. Whether it be connecting to the journey we took with the progression of Mom's Alzheimer's disease or the affirmation of knowing there is something far greater and more wonderful than we could ever imagine waiting for us after this life, we hope you've found some sense of peace you didn't possess before reading this book.

When I had first retired from my career, I knew I needed a break from the years I had spent in education, but I also knew I wanted to find some new sense of purpose. As I lay awake one night, I was asking God to provide me with some sort of message or direction as I was at a complete loss of what the next steps for me could and should look like. As I lay there, I have no doubt He clearly spoke to me as the idea of the book literally came out of nowhere. I had never written anything before that wasn't required for my education or communication purposes at work, so it was a little scary at first. I also knew God wouldn't ask anything of me unless He knew I could do it. I felt as if He were saying to me that it would be a shame to have all of these experiences and knowledge and hang on to it in a tightly closed fist. Why not share it with others who might need to hear exactly what you have to say?

Were there times I wanted to quit Absolutely! As I wrote the words on the pages, some of it was painfully difficult to relive and remember. I would call Dad when I would be unsure how to convey something or if I just needed affirmation that what I was doing was focused on communicating Mom's story and honoring her memory. I know this wasn't easy for him either, but he never turned down an opportunity to hear what I had written. He patiently listened and always provided me with actionable feedback. This book was something we truly both embarked on together. I also would reach out to God if I felt I had hit a wall or thought there was no way I could actually finish writing a book. Each time I did, I found the continued strength to press on and let go of any doubt that had tried to seep into my mind.

My dad and I miss Mom every day. Of course, some days are better than others, but we are both thankful we spent some wonderful years with her and have many memories to treasure. I think of her each time I drive through and get an ice cream cone, place a pair of her embroidered pillow cases on the pillows when changing the sheets, or when I make her potato salad, which I promise took several years to master. I picture her on the back porch swing visiting with friends and family when I pull up to the house to visit with my Dad. She's everywhere, and that's a good thing because there are so many good things to remember. In my prayers at night, I always ask God to tell her hello for me as I imagine she's far too busy in heaven reconnecting and reminiscing with friends and family. I look forward to the day when I, too, can go to my heavenly home and hear the words once again, "There you are"!

About the Author

Beth M. Hamilton is a retired educator who spent time as a classroom teacher, media specialist, and assistant principal. She and her husband Jim are residents of Columbia, Tennessee, and are the parents of one grown son. This is Beth's first book, which she wrote after finding the strength from God and the support of her family and friends to share her mom's story.

Made in United States
Cleveland, OH
22 August 2025